College Success for Adults

College Success for Adults: Insider Tips for Effective Learning is a concise, user-friendly guide to college success for the *adult* college student. In it, readers learn to master the rules, vocabulary, and expectations of the college environment. They'll discover how to balance their work and personal lives with college-level study, develop the mindset of the successful college student, take notes effectively, conquer testing anxiety, win over their professors, and much more.

Armed with the knowledge this book provides, readers will emerge with a deeper understanding of what it takes to succeed in college—and how *they* can achieve this success. They'll learn how to take their own experience and wisdom as adults and translate it into success in the college classroom. Readers also receive helpful supplementary resources that will aid them on their journey to college success, including a college vocabulary glossary, college knowledge quiz (with answer key), a list of scholarships exclusively for adult students, and a suggested course syllabus (with detailed course calendar).

C.M. Gill is on the faculty at Austin Community College in Austin, TX, where she enjoys teaching adult students in her College Success, English, and math courses. As the Supervisor of ACC's College Prep Program for seven years, she helped thousands of adult students transition successfully into college.

College Success for Adults
Insider Tips for Effective Learning

C.M. Gill

Routledge
Taylor & Francis Group

NEW YORK AND LONDON

First published 2021
by Routledge
52 Vanderbilt Avenue, New York, NY 10017

and by Routledge
2 Park Square, Milton Park, Abingdon, Oxon, OX14 4RN

Routledge is an imprint of the Taylor & Francis Group, an informa business

© 2021 Taylor & Francis

Library of Congress Cataloging-in-Publication Data
Names: Gill, C. M. (Charlene M.), author.
Title: College success for adults: insider tips for effective learning / C.M. Gill.
Description: New York, NY: Routledge, 2021. | Includes bibliographical references and index.
Identifiers: LCCN 2020009416 (print) | LCCN 2020009417 (ebook) | ISBN 9780367466800 (hardback) | ISBN 9780367466794 (paperback) | ISBN 9781003030324 (ebook)
Subjects: LCSH: Adult college students–United States–Handbooks, manuals, etc. | College student orientation–United States–Handbooks, manuals, etc. | Adult learning–United States–Handbooks, manuals, etc.
Classification: LCC LC5251 .G55 2021 (print) | LCC LC5251 (ebook) | DDC 374/.973–dc23
LC record available at https://lccn.loc.gov/2020009416
LC ebook record available at https://lccn.loc.gov/2020009417

ISBN: 978-0-367-46680-0 (hbk)
ISBN: 978-0-367-46679-4 (pbk)
ISBN: 978-1-003-03032-4 (ebk)

Typeset in Sabon
by Deanta Global Publishing Services, Chennai, India

For My Students—Past, Present, and Future

Contents

About the Author

C.M. Gill graduated Phi Beta Kappa and with highest honors from the University of Texas at Austin—while working full time to put herself through school. She was a member of the psychology honor society Psi Chi, The Golden Key National Honor Society, and Who's Who. After earning her undergraduate degree, she went on to graduate school and earned an MA from Texas State University where she became a member of the English honor society Sigma Tau Delta, was named an Outstanding Graduate Student, and joined the teaching faculty of the English Department.

Since then, she's won numerous teaching and writing awards and currently enjoys teaching adult students in her College Success, English, and math courses at Austin Community College in Austin, TX. One of her favorite professional roles here was serving as the Supervisor of the College Prep Program for seven years. In this role, she helped thousands of adult students make a successful transition from the home, workplace, or GED classroom into college. She has also taught GED, developmental reading and writing, and English Composition classes.

She is the author of the college writing textbook, *Essential Writing Skills for College and Beyond* (Penguin, 2014), and the program management handbook, *Un-Rig the Game: Empower Adult Students for Success in College* (Scribble Fire, 2017). In her spare time, she writes plays, TV shows, novels, and other fun works of fiction. She hopes to spend more time reading soon.

Preface

This book began in my College Prep Program as my students and I searched for a guide to college success for adult students.

What we found wasn't exactly helpful. Most books were written for an audience of 18-year-old university freshmen living in a dorm. They offered "tips" such as how to decorate your dorm on the cheap, party all night and still get As, land an internship while studying abroad, and (my personal favorite!) how to turn a bed sheet into a toga.

While the toga example is definitely funny, advice like this is not exactly what most adult students are seeking in a college success book. They work full time, have kids, and are coming back to school for the first time in years. They simply want help navigating the system and understanding the rules.

They want a book that answers questions like these:

- How much do classes cost—and how/where can I get help to pay for them?
- Where can I find a "cheat sheet" on the vocabulary of the college world?
- How can I balance work, kids, *and* school—and still succeed?
- How do I make sure I get a good, stable job after graduation?
- What are some ways I can overcome math and test anxiety?
- Are there shortcuts or "best practices" for studying?
- What do my professors expect of me and what can I expect of them?

Since we couldn't find a book that answered these questions, I started compiling this information for my students.

It was so helpful to them that they insisted I put it all together into a book for future students.

The book you have in your hand (or on your screen!) *is* that book.

My goal in writing it is that it will empower you, the adult student, to gain the skills, knowledge, tools, and confidence you need for success in college.

I hope this book will inspire you to begin envisioning this success for yourself *each* day. This is critical to do, because if you don't see this success for yourself, you probably won't believe you can achieve it. And, if you don't believe you'll achieve it, you probably won't.

So, why not start right now?
Go ahead. Envision yourself succeeding in college.
See that successful grade report.
Imagine yourself walking across that stage.

Feel the surge of excitement you'll experience when you're applying for that dream job—and eventually landing it.

Go on. See it. Feel it. (I'll wait...)
When you're ready, turn the page, and let's get started in moving you toward that vision.

Acknowledgments

I'd like to express my deep gratitude first and foremost to my students—past, present, and future. This book would not exist without them. Their support, encouragement, and hard work have inspired me beyond words, and I cannot thank you enough.

I'd also like to thank my mother, Robin; my father, Charles; and my sister, Kimberly, who were among my first teachers. Without them, I could never have written this book, or any other. Thank you for your support and encouragement. To my incredible nephews—Tyler, Alex, Dylan, and Silas—you make life fun, exciting, and always new. Thank you. And, to Thomas for always being my number one fan—thank you for believing in me and inspiring my work. I couldn't do this with you.

Thank you to my incredible editor, Matthew Friberg. Without your help and insight propelling me forward, this project would probably still be sitting in a drawer, never to see the light. Thanks also to Jessica Cooke, my amazing editorial assistant, who answered my never-ending list of questions.

Thank you to my friend and colleague, Nadine Cooper, who saw the promise in this book early, and helped me to keep believing in it.

Thank you to my colleagues for their never-ending support and inspiration: David Borden, Kathy Dowdy, Linda Munoz, Patricia Hernandez, William Perry, Sunita Misra, Deloris Collins, Richard Looney, Michele Donnelly, Debbie Talavera, Barbara Rotolo-Caballero, Susan Gusler, Jason Katz, Allison Mosshart, Katherine Garrett, Ted Rachofsky, Lisa Carlo, Griselda Valerio, Tonya Lyles, Sharon Frederick, Dorado Kinney, Jodi Denyszyn, Mieca Johnson, Jessica Listi, Mechelle Marler, Cheryl Thompson Price, Charles Floyd, Lillian Huerta, Irene Miller, Jason Brown, Gloria Dove-Owens, Sherry Prather, Susan Gusler, Cynthia La, Sonia Hogan, Karen Cook, Emily Payne, and Mary Helen Martinez.

Special thanks to my beta readers who helped shape this book—and made it much, much better: Kathy Dowdy, Sunita Misra, Ted Stanhope, Maricela Juarez, Mary Helen Martinez, Sandra Akhlaque, Mieca Johnson, and David Borden.

Introduction

I'd like to open this book by addressing two of the most frequently asked questions I hear from incoming adult college students:

1) Can I really succeed in college—at *my* age?!
2) Is college even worth the time, effort, and money?

Please allow me to end the debate to the first question right now. The answer is undoubtedly: **Yes!** You can absolutely go to college and succeed.

How do I know?

Over the last decade, I've worked with thousands of adult students starting college for the first time or returning after many, many years. These students all shared the same worries: Will they be the oldest student in the class? Were they smart enough, good enough, or quick enough to do the work? Were they adequately prepared by their high school or GED classes?

I'm happy to share with you their good news: These students did indeed succeed, and still are succeeding, in their college classes.

In fact, most of them are now straight-A Honors students who are among the best students in their classes and schools.

These are students who are probably just like you—they were out of the classroom for years, some for decades. They have children, parents, and even grandparents they are taking care of, and they work full time.

Yet, they have succeeded—and so can you.

I know you can succeed because you already share with these amazing students the number one trait associated with success in college—*determination*. These students are incredibly successful because they were determined to succeed. They did the work required. They persisted when it was hard. They pushed past the numerous barriers that tried to stop them.

And you will, too.

How do I know? I know because you care so much about succeeding in college and are so serious about it that you found and picked up this book—and you're actually reading it! Only a serious, highly dedicated student would do that.

Let's now turn to that second question you may be asking yourself: Is college even worth the time and effort?

With all the uproar in the media regarding the value of a college degree, many people are starting to wonder if college is even worth all the effort and money. This is indeed a valid question.

Yet, before we look at any statistics, it's important you understand that no one else can answer that question for you. I can share with you what the data shows about college graduates and their success versus those with only a high school diploma. Yet, the truth is that *only you* can determine whether or not college is worth the cost to you and your family.

College costs money, yes, but it costs you something else, too: your time, effort, and energy.

If you're looking for a guarantee that college will make you a zillionaire, I can't offer you that. (Sorry!) However, even though college may not make you rich, it will undoubtedly make you rich*er,* in every sense of the word—academically, professionally, personally, and, yes, financially.

In college, you'll acquire knowledge, skills, and abilities you may not even realize you have, and it will bring out of you power, talent, capabilities, and confidence that will translate to any and every environment you'll encounter—for the rest of your life.

Getting yourself a college education also benefits your kids, friends, neighbors, and entire community. Listen to what Bill Gates (the founder of Microsoft, and one of the wealthiest people on earth) says about going to college:

> College graduates are more likely to find a rewarding job, earn higher income, and even live healthier, happier lives than if they didn't have degrees. They also bring training and skills into America's work force, helping our economy grow and stay competitive... It's just too bad that we're not producing more of them.[1]
>
> (Bill Gates quoted in Leonhardt,
> *The New York Times* 2015)

And, happily, the research shows Mr. Gates is right. Below are some of the benefits that research[2] shows you gain with a college credential:

- **More Money**
  - Annual earnings are about 134% higher.
- **Less Poverty**
  - The incidence of poverty is 3.5 times lower.
- **More Health Insurance**
  - The likelihood of having health insurance through employment is 47% higher.
- **More Retirement**
  - Retirement income is 2.4 times higher.

- **More Job Safety**
  - The incidence of receiving workers' compensation is 2.4 times lower.
- **Less Unemployment**
  - The likelihood of being out of the labor force is 74% less
- **More Health and Happiness**
  - Health and happiness reported as "very good" or "excellent" is 44% higher (Trostel 2).

The truth is that getting a college education is probably the safest investment you can make. It's something no one can ever steal from you, and it is the closest you can get to a guarantee of financial and professional success.

The only catch is that it's a great deal of work. It will require you to become adept at doing many things you may never have done before, or may not have done in a long time.

That's where this book comes in.

In it, you'll discover the 14 steps needed to get you from start to finish—from starting that college class to graduating—and beyond.

We'll cover topics such as:

- Developing the mindset of the successful college student
- Mastering the rules, etiquette, and vocabulary of the college world (academia)
- Studying *smarter*—not harder
- Saving money on books and tuition, and winning grants and scholarships
- Acing tests and conquering testing anxiety
- Achieving balance in going to school, raising kids, and working
- Finding and landing your ideal career—and even earn promotions

---

And much, much more.

You'll also receive an Appendix of supplemental materials, including a glossary of college vocabulary terms, a list of scholarships exclusively for adult students, tips on how to transfer to a university, and a college knowledge quiz (with answer key!).

Feel free to read the book cover to cover, or just flip to the chapters that you feel are most important to you right now.

If you're brand new to college, you may want to begin with Appendix A, which provides you with a glossary of academic vocabulary terms. We will use these terms throughout this book to help you begin learning them.

However, you're welcome and encouraged to use this book as you see fit so that it works for *you*. The main thing is to get started and on your way. So, turn the page, and let's get going.

Notes

1 Read the full article by David Leonhardt here: https://nytimes.com/2015/06/04/upshot/bill-gates-college-dropout-dont-be-like-me.html
2 Read the full article by Philip Trostel here: https://luminafoundation.org/files/resources/its-not-just-the-money.pdf

Section I

Building a Strong Foundation for Your Success

1 Develop the Mindset of a Successful College Student

IN THIS CHAPTER, YOU WILL LEARN:

- Why some students succeed in college, and others do not
- How to develop the mindset of a successful college student
- How to overcome your fears of going back to school

Let's open this chapter with a question:

Why do some students succeed in college, but others do not?

As a new college student, you've probably asked yourself this question, perhaps many times. So, what's the answer?

When I ask my students what they think, without fail, they always give some very insightful responses. Here's what they say:

Successful Students:

- Show up for class regularly and participate actively
- Do the homework
- Study faithfully and consistently
- Make sacrifices
- Don't give up, even when it gets hard
- Are courageous and brave
- Learn from mistakes
- Take advantage of resources
- Take classes seriously
- Get help when they need it

Unsuccessful Students:

- Basically do the opposite of the above list

The students make some good points with this list above, but as you read it, I would wager you are not exactly surprised by it.

Most people understand that to succeed in college, you must work hard, go to class, study, make sacrifices, etc., but what few people understand is *why* all students do not do those things.

Often, they think it is because some students are lazy or they just don't "want it" enough. Perhaps that's true for a few students, but I've found that most students really *want* to succeed in college. They may not necessarily *want* to study for hours every week or sacrifice personal time to join a study group, but they're willing to do it. Yet, even still, these students do not always succeed.

The question is: why not?

The problem lies in that long list of traits, the one at the top of this chapter. If you found it a bit overwhelming, you're not alone. Most of us feel this way when given a long list of traits we must cultivate to succeed. It's easy to tell people *what* to do and not give them any idea of how to do it, and therein lies the root of many students' issues in college: They know *what* to do, but they don't know *how* to do it.

It's easy for me to tell you to study hard for your college classes; that's not exactly a revelation from the heavens. Yet, teaching you *how* to study for them might just be, because most students do not know yet how to study successfully.

So, that is what you'll learn in this chapter and beyond—not merely *what* to do, but *how* to do it so you have a roadmap to success.

The first step on the road to that success begins not with learning to study or how to take tests or ways to manage your time. We'll get to those topics, but we must first start at the beginning, which is your mindset—specifically with developing a **growth mindset** and rejecting **a fixed mindset**.

Growth vs. Fixed Mindsets

The terms "growth mindset" and "fixed mindset" were developed by Dr. Carol Dweck of Stanford University. She spent decades studying thousands of students, from kindergarten through graduate school, to discover why some students succeed and others do not. What she discovered was that success lies in the mind—and so does failure. It all depends on the student's mindset because all students, whether they realize it or not, have one of two mindsets: a **fixed** or a **growth** mindset.

What is the difference between the two mindsets?

The Fixed Mindset

A person with a fixed mindset believes talent, intelligence, and abilities are fixed at birth. They see abilities as innate, meaning they cannot be changed with effort, practice, or persistence.

In other words, fixed-mindset people believe we're born with a certain amount of intelligence and ability, and there is nothing we can do to change it.

The Growth Mindset

A person with a growth mindset understands that although some people may be born with more natural intelligence or abilities in certain subjects than other people, these abilities are *not* fixed for life. Instead, intelligence and skills can be grown and developed with effort, practice, and persistence.

In other words, growth-mindset people know that we can grow and expand our intelligence and abilities with practice, hard word, and persistence.

Think about these mindsets and how they might work in the mind of a college student.

Do you think fixed or growth mindset students are more successful? Why?

If you said students with a growth mindset are significantly more successful, you're correct—and this proves true regardless of gender, age, or socioeconomic background.

In fact, Dr. Dweck and her research team discovered that having a growth mindset predicted higher final grades in difficult college courses (such as organic chemistry), and it also predicted the student's ability to successfully recover from mistakes and failures (Grant & Dweck 2003).

If you're starting to worry that maybe you have a fixed mindset and you're doomed for failure, don't worry; Dr. Dweck has good news on this front:

We can easily switch from a fixed to a growth mindset.

This switch is indeed good news since our society tends to encourage us to have a fixed mindset, which is why so many of us probably do begin college with a fixed mindset. Since this is the case, let's begin there, with the fixed mindset, so we can understand how this mindset works and the ways we see the world through its lens.

The Fixed Mindset

Imagine a baby sitting on a bed, holding an Einstein book on the theory of relativity.

The baby is squinting, trying to understand, but she just can't quite get it.

Then, an adult enters the room and sees the baby struggling to read the Einstein book.

Rather than being impressed or charmed by the baby's effort, this adult points her finger at the baby and mocks her, saying something such as, "You stupid baby! What a moron you are. You should just hang it up! You'll NEVER learn that. You're just not smart enough. If you were, you would already understand it."

The adult then shakes her head in disgust and leaves the room.

I hope you're appalled by this adult's reaction to and treatment of this child. It's a made-up scenario, thankfully, but it contains a kernel of truth in that it's what so many of us think, perhaps not about anyone else, but we often think it of ourselves.

Most of us would never respond in this mean-spirited, defeating way to someone else trying to learn something new.

Yet, how many of us berate ourselves when we are learning something new and don't instantly catch on?

How many of us call ourselves names (such as "stupid" or "idiot") when we're trying to understand new material or working to develop new skills and we're not quite getting there?

For example, think about the last time you attempted a difficult problem in your most challenging class.

What did your internal dialogue sound like? Did you get angry at yourself? Did you call yourself names? Did you conclude you were "stupid" or "hopeless" at that subject or activity?

If so, you were just channeling the fixed mindset.

Sadly, we most likely learned this behavior from our society, which encourages the belief that if you're not instantly good at something, you never will be.

We often praise athletes, musicians, and other celebrities whom we're assured are "naturals," and rarely do we hear about the hours, years, or even decades these so-called "naturals" spent practicing and honing their skills.

We even have many cultural sayings that encourage the fixed mindset. You've probably heard many of these, or even perhaps said them yourself. These fixed-mindset sayings include:

- "I'm just not a math person."
- "I'll never be a great writer."
- "Science is too hard for me."
- "I'm so disorganized—always have been, always will be."
- "I'm just not good at school."
- "You've either got it, or you don't."

That last statement, "You've either got it, or you don't," expresses the essence of the fixed mindset.

> **People with a fixed mindset believe that success is created by inherent talent—*not* effort**

The fixed mindset tells us that college is about proving how smart we already are, not *becoming* smarter.

Therefore, people with a fixed mindset see effort as pointless. After all, they reason, if you have to try, you must not "have it," so why even bother?

As a result of this belief, fixed mindset people spend their time trying to *prove* their intelligence and talents instead of *developing* and *growing* them.

When they aren't instantly good at something, they conclude they just "don't have 'it'" in that particular activity or area, so they want to quickly move on since they believe they can't possibly improve.

They also fear their lack of mastery will make them appear "dumb," either to themselves or to others, so they avoid challenges, lest anyone think they are not "smart."

This mindset will almost certainly ensure *disaster* for a college student because:

College requires you to grow your intelligence.

College students will face many, many challenges, and if they quit everything they're not instantly good at doing, they won't make it through to graduation.

The good news, though, is that with a growth mindset, you'll start seeing those challenges differently, and you'll start overcoming them through the power of your belief, determination, and hard work—and, as a result, you'll become stronger and smarter.

The Growth Mindset

The **growth mindset** is one that understands intelligence is *not* fixed, that it is changeable through effort, practice, diligence, and hard work.

> Growth mindset people know that by taking on challenging new tasks, they **make their brains smarter.**

Dr. Dweck's research shows that the brain works like a muscle, meaning the more we work it out (by studying and learning new things), the smarter we get.

Most people understand that *children* get smarter as they learn, but most of us were not taught that we ourselves can get smarter as adults. Yet, research shows that this is exactly the case: We can actually increase our intelligence.

Yes, you read that correctly: Research has demonstrated that adults can grow their intelligence by learning new things, especially challenging new things.

We can and do make ourselves smarter by learning new things.

Since the brain works like a muscle, it gets stronger and works better the more it is exercised. So, every time you stretch yourself by working hard and learning something new, your brain forms new connections and, over time, you become smarter (Grant & Dweck 2003).

Think of learning new things as the mental equivalent of working out, making your brain grow stronger.

The Challenge

I wish I could say that Dr. Dweck's research shows that all of this learning will be quick, easy, and painless. Unfortunately, it's just the opposite! All this learning will take time, be difficult, and sometimes even painful.

This is the part where most people give up.

Learning something new is difficult, and takes time to master, so when someone doesn't instantly get it, they assume it's too hard for them, and they quit.

This is when you need to do *more* work, not less. When a subject is hard, give it *more* time. Put in even *more* effort. (Don't worry; we'll discuss *how* to do that successfully in Chapters 7, 8, 9, 10, and 12!)

Slowly, the material will start getting easier because you're "working out" your brain in that area.

Granted, this is easier said than done, but that is what it means to have a growth mindset: You understand that **acquiring new knowledge takes effort and hard work.**

Remember, no one just magically knows how to solve quadratic equations or write essays or add fractions. Everyone who knows how to do these things had to be *taught*. They had to learn it.

So, when you enter your college classes, keep that fact in mind.

You will *not* know everything the instructor will teach you. If you did, what would be the point of going to class?!

You're in college to *learn*, so if you see a calendar filled with items you do not know yet, that is good news! It means you're going to learn a lot of new information that semester and become a lot smarter!

The first few challenges will most likely be the hardest, but the good news is that it will get easier the more you do it.

One Final Point: On "Smart" and "Dumb"

Most of us were probably taught that people are born either "smart" or "dumb." We can be "smart" in English but "dumb" in math, this so-called wisdom claims.

You've probably heard people crack "jokes" such as, "The Good Lord just didn't see fit to give me math abilities!", or "I was out sick the day God was handing out writing talent!"

These so-called jokes are not the least bit funny because the speaker is giving him or herself permission to remain limited and never grow in those areas.

Additionally, these statements are factually incorrect.

We *all* can become better in every subject, no matter what our current skill level.

Granted, it will probably be more work for us than it is for someone who might have a bit more natural gifting in that area than we do, but, still, we can do it.

This is why it's critical you not compare yourself to anyone else while you make your way through your classes. If your fellow students seem to be catching on to a concept faster than you are, this does not mean they are "smart" and you are "dumb." It simply means they may have more training and education in this area than you do, or it means they've practiced longer, or perhaps they have more innate abilities in this particular area. By no means does that mean you are "dumb."

In fact, Dr. Dweck's research has shown that this old idea of "smart" and "dumb" is inaccurate.

No one is either "smart" or "dumb."

We are either challenging ourselves and growing our intelligence in certain areas (such as math, science, English, etc.), or we're not. If we're not challenging ourselves, that does <u>not</u> mean that we are "dumb." It simply means we have not challenged ourselves in that subject yet.

This is indeed the key word: <u>YET</u> – We *can* learn it. We just haven't learned it yet.

Simply because you were not good at algebra in junior high does not mean you cannot learn it now, in college. You can.

It may be true that right now you have no idea how to solve a complex calculus problem, speak a foreign language, or write a persuasive essay. That's okay. That's why you're here, in college, is it not? You're here to learn how to do those things. If you already knew how to do them, then why would you be here?

You may not know how to do those things **YET**, but you will.

Think about all the things you didn't know how to do at one time that were really, really hard to learn (such as walking, speaking, reading, writing, etc.) Yet, you learned to do all of those things and thousands of others.

Now, as an adult, you have even *more* intelligence, experience, and knowledge than you did when you acquired those skills, and you can use those abilities to help you acquire the ones you need for college, too. It will just take work, effort, and persistence—and *belief*.

If you don't believe you can grow your abilities, you're not likely to try to do so. That is one of the key essences of the growth mindset—it points to the power of your *beliefs*.

> **"For they can conquer who <u>believe</u> they can"**
> —John Dryden (emphasis mine)

What Dryden meant was this: **Success starts with your thinking.**

If you decide you can't do something, then you're not likely to work hard at doing it.

After all, if it can't be done, then what's the point of working hard?

Yet, if you believe deep within you that you can do something, you're much more likely to work hard to do it.

This point brings us back to the question posed at the beginning of this chapter and why some students succeed while others do not.

I bet you know the answer now: Successful college students develop a growth mindset.

They understand that they can and will become smarter and more highly skilled, but only with effort and practice.

That's what goes wrong with so many students who never finish college. It's not that they *couldn't* do it; it's that they give up because they didn't *believe* they could.

When they faced challenges in their classes, they assumed it meant they weren't college material, that they weren't smart enough. So, they gave up.

It's not that they were lazy or didn't care; it's just that they didn't see the challenges in the right light. They thought the challenges meant they didn't know the material, so that's the end. They didn't realize the challenges meant they didn't know the material **yet**.

So, sadly, they let those challenges overcome them, instead of working hard to overcome the challenges.

As you make your way through your classes, remember that the ways in which you view the challenges thrown your way will determine whether you overcome them or not.

When you experience failures or mistakes, remember that they are actually good news because they are proof that you are stretching yourself and trying something new.

They mean that you're growing.

You may not be succeeding in that subject **yet**, but you will. Struggle is just part of the process. It's a step on the way to success, a required one.

To go into the world and try new things takes bravery and courage and heart, so keep on trying, and eventually you *will* get better, but **only** if you keep trying.

The only real failure is to never try.

On the page below, you will find a re-cap of the two mindsets from Dr. Dweck's fantastic book, *Mindset: The New Psychology of Success*.

I encourage you to read or listen to her book and check in with yourself regularly to see: Are you displaying a growth or a fixed mindset?

GROWTH *Mindset*	FIXED *Mindset*
• Intelligence is not fixed; you can become smarter by studying and working hard	• Intelligence is fixed; we're all either "smart" or "dumb," and there's nothing anyone can do about it
• We can become smarter and learn new, challenging things with effort and hard work	• You can learn new things that are easy, but you can't actually get smarter
• If you weren't born with "it," you can learn and develop "it" (could be math, writing, whatever)	• You've either "got it," or you don't, and there's nothing you can do to change that fact
• No one is born a "math person"; everyone who is good at math had to study and work hard, and every person (barring a brain injury) can learn math	• You're either a "math person" or you're not—and there's nothing you can do about it
• Some people may be born with more natural intelligence or ability in some areas than other people, but with study and practice, we will increase our skills and become smarter	• If you aren't instantly good at something, that means you just don't have talent in that area, and you never will

What is the difference in the two groups of people?

GROWTH *Mindset People*	FIXED *Mindset People*
• Listen to helpful feedback and grow and learn from it • Face challenges and persist through them • Care more about *learning* than always trying to look "smart" • See other people's success as inspiring • Grow and become smarter and smarter	• Ignore feedback and don't grow or learn • Avoid challenges • Care more about *looking* smart than *becoming* smarter • See other people's success as a threat, and often compare themselves to others • Stay pretty much the same

Suggested Exercise

1) Write about your mindsets regarding education—past, present, and future. Some questions you may want to consider:
   - When you studied (no matter what the subject was—math, science, writing, etc.), how did you talk to yourself about the subject(s)?
   - When the work became challenging, you would say____.
   - When the work was easy for you, you would say _____.
2) Write about your teachers, parents, and/or anyone whose mindsets may have affected yours. Some questions you may want to consider:
   - Did parents or teachers often praise you for being "smart" when you got problems or questions correct?
   - Did parents or teachers insult you or call you "dumb" (or worse) when you got problems or questions incorrect?
   - When you noticed other students who were "good" at certain subjects or skills, did you think they were just born with some magical ability, or did you understand that they worked at it?
3) Write about how you plan to improve your mindset, this semester and beyond, particularly when facing academic challenges. Some questions you may want to consider:
   - When you face challenges in your classes, what will you say to yourself?
   - Be specific. When you want to quit or give up when something is challenging for you, what specifically will you do to persist and be successful?
4) Share your answers with a partner and/or friend/family member. Get them to share their own experiences, and brainstorm together how you can help each other to adopt a growth mindset.

Instead of writing about your experiences, feel free to draw, paint, rap, or sing to process and learn from them.

2 The Top 10 Myths about College You Must Not Believe

IN THIS CHAPTER, YOU WILL LEARN:

- The most frequently held myths new students often believe about college
- What is true—and not true—about college and why it's crucial you know the difference

When I meet with new college students, they are often frustrated and stressed because they have heard so much conflicting information about college that they're not sure what to believe. "What is the *truth*??", they want to know.

In this chapter, we'll cover the myths you've probably heard about college and go over how and why they're not true. This is crucial to do, too, because some of these myths are so pervasive and destructive that students who believe them often give up on college entirely or never even make it to their first day.

To get started, let's first see how much you already know regarding myths about college life. Take the quick quiz on the following page. On it, you'll find statements about college. Mark each either "true" or "false."

Be honest here, too!

COLLEGE MYTH QUIZ

1. **True/False**. Adult students don't really belong in college; academically speaking, they just can't compete with the younger students.
2. **True/False**. College is really, really expensive and without a doubt will put you in hundreds of thousands of dollars of debt.
3. **True/False**. Lots of people are financially and professionally successful without a college credential.

4. **True/False**. You have to be really, really smart—almost a genius—to do well in college.
5. **True/False**. Professors often embarrass students in class, and enjoy doing so.
6. **True/False**. College is zero tolerance; one mistake, and you're finished!
7. **True/False** You have to give up *everything* else in your life during college if you want to do well.
8. **True/False**. In college, you're on your own; no one will help you.
9. **True/False**. College is a competition; it's me against the other students.
10. **True/False**. Most college students know *exactly* what they want to do with their lives.

Here's the answer key: Every statement above is false.

Now, let's go over each one so you will understand *why* they are false and what, exactly, is the truth.

MYTH #1: Adult Students Don't Really Belong in College; Academically Speaking, They Just Can't Compete with the Younger Students

Adult students often believe this myth, citing the old adage, "You can't teach an old dog new tricks." They then use this "wisdom" to claim that younger students are and always will be better, smarter students.

Yet, the research shows this simply is not true.

To begin, there are two critical points to understand regarding the axiom around "old dogs:"

(1) Actually, psychologists have demonstrated that we can indeed teach "old dogs new tricks," and
(2) You are a *human being*, not a dog. So, even if teaching "old dogs new tricks" was not possible, this analogy still would not be an apt one to apply to human beings.

So, let's begin with the psychologists and the "old dogs."

A group of psychologists at the University of Vienna conducted a three-year-long study with dogs who were up to 13 years old (an age considered "old" in dogs).

Here's what the psychologists found: The older dogs actually out-performed the younger dogs in several key areas of the study—including logical reasoning, which the researchers concluded, *improves* with age!

In fact, one of the researchers, Dr. Friederike Range, concluded: "The older the dog, the better it performed" (Coren 2016)[1].

Researchers at Dartmouth University were intrigued by this study and wanted to see if the findings held true in *humans* as well. In other words, just because we can teach old *dogs* new tricks, does this mean we can teach adult humans "new tricks," too?!

If you read Chapter 1 on mindset, you already know the answer: it's a resounding yes.

The Dartmouth researchers found that the adult brain is just as capable of learning and expanding as younger brains. Here's how they put it: The adult brain retains "a robust capacity for reorganization with learning. Like a muscle that grows with use, the brain appears capable of expanding the functionality of networks involved in learning" (Schlegel 1669).

Here's what this research means: It shows that as an "older" student, you have no disadvantage, neurologically speaking!

The one catch with this study was that the researchers found that adult brains do sometimes require a few more trials to reinforce learning than younger brains do. In other words, the adult brains needed a few more practices than the younger brains.

So, if you notice younger students catching on faster than you do, just remember that this is expected and nothing to worry about.

Also, remember that as an adult student, you have several advantages:

- **You've acquired invaluable life experiences that will help you in college**
  - Your experiences have given you wisdom and understanding that most younger students just haven't had the chance to develop yet.
  - You've already solved many, many problems and gone through situations that are much more complicated to solve than many of the problems you'll encounter in your classes.
- **You already know college will take sacrifices and hard work**
  - As an adult student, you don't need a lecture on how you shouldn't stay out all night partying and then come to class the next day hungover to take a test. You already understand this fact and know that you must study and work hard, and this understanding empowers you to succeed.
- **You are a hard worker**
  - As an adult student, you're probably a parent and/or employee, which means you're not afraid of hard work, and it means that you understand what commitment and teamwork are. It also means you know how to manage your time better than you probably think.
- **Your educational past will serve you well**
  - All students have an educational past, but adult students often have had more time (and sometimes more serious life reasons) to reflect

upon that past than younger students. Thus, adult students are often in a better position to really understand the value of what they've learned from those experiences. They know what worked, what didn't, and how these experiences can be transformed into powerful lessons that inspire the student to greater and greater heights of success.

- **You are highly motivated**
  - As an adult student, you probably already understand too well the consequences of life without a college credential, and you likely *do not* want to keep experiencing them in the future. You can tap into this knowledge (and perhaps frustration!) as a powerful motivator to keep going when classes become challenging.
- **You are *choosing* to be in college**
  - Most likely, you are in college because you choose to be; your parents or guardians are not forcing you to go to school, which means you will almost certainly take your classes very seriously. This is a huge asset for you, not only because it means you'll enjoy your coursework and appreciate your education, but also because it is a trait professors notice—and reward.

For all these reasons, you are highly likely to succeed in your classes—that is, if you keep working and refuse to give up.

Remind yourself to keep your eye on the "prize" so to speak, meaning keep in mind *why* you're in college and what it will do for you. That focus will help you to persevere when you face challenges.

MYTH #2: College Is *Super* Expensive and Without a Doubt Will Put You into Hundreds of Thousands of Dollars of Debt

This myth is often advanced by well-meaning people who hope to "educate" students on the so-called high costs of college. The truth, however, is that college—much more often than not—pays for itself many times over.

And, beyond that, the actual cost of a college education is not as high as many people believe.

The outrageously high costs that many sensationalized media stories highlight (such as stories of students with several hundred thousand dollars of debt!) usually are so high because the student earned a high-level degree, such as a doctorate or medical degree.

The truth is that how much you spend on college will depend on what degree(s) you earn and what school(s) you attend.

If you go to Harvard to get a medical degree, then, yes, you probably will acquire a great deal of debt! However, if you attend a community college or state university to get an associate or bachelor's degree, then you probably won't acquire much, if any, debt.

So, instead of listening to sensationalized speculation on how "expensive" college is, do your own research and discover how much your education will actually cost.

Another important point to remember regarding this myth is that it assumes students must necessarily go into debt to attain a college education, and that is simply not true, either.

You may have to get a student loan, but you may not. We'll also cover cost and how to get free money for your education in Chapter 4, but for now, read and understand the following facts about student loan debt:

FACT A: *You may not have to go into debt at all because there are many sources of educational funding available.*

There are *many* other sources of money for which you can apply that do not require re-payment or interest, such as the federal financial aid student grant, which can give you up to $6,195 per year. This is funding you can apply to books, fees, and tuition—and you do not have to pay it back, so long as you attend and pass your classes.

In addition, as an adult student in particular, you have several other funding options open to you. You can find a list of suggested resources in Appendix B, but, for now, just know that you do have options for financing your education *other than* student loans. These options include:

• Grants (federal, state, and local)
• Scholarships
• Work-Study
• Employer subsidies

It's well worth your time to look into these options, so do your homework on these before signing on the dotted line for a loan. (Also, see Chapter 4.)

If you still have questions, don't hesitate to reach out to your financial aid office. It's their job to help you, so don't feel like you're bothering them. You're not!

FACT B: *The vast majority of students benefit greatly from the money they invest in earning a college credential.*

One of the main reasons most students go to college is so they can earn more money in their future careers. Yet, media hype causes many people to worry about whether college is even worth it anymore.

If you, too, are worried about this question, I have good news: the research indicates the answer is almost certainly "yes."

Granted, no one can honestly guarantee you 100% that earning a college credential will absolutely, certainly, ensure you earn more money. Yet, your chances of increasing your earnings with a college degree are *almost* certain.

Here's what the research shows[2]:

- A high school dropout earns $973,000 over a lifetime.
- A high school diploma holder earns $1.3 million over a lifetime.
- A worker with some college (but no degree) earns $1.5 million over a lifetime.
- An associate degree-holder earns $1.7 million over a lifetime.
- A bachelor's degree-holder earns $2.3 million over a lifetime.
- A master's degree-holder earns $2.7 million over a lifetime.

See the pattern?

More education = more money.

Notice that even the worker who did not *complete* college but received *some* college increased his earnings by $200,000. Even if he had to pay $10,000 to get that education, he'd make roughly $190,000 in profit, less any interest he may have to pay. (But it's unlikely it would cost him $10,000 to get just a few college credits! It would likely cost much, much less than that!)

The Federal Reserve Bank of San Francisco agrees. They reported that the average college graduate earns "over *$800,000 more* than the average high school graduate by retirement age" (Daly & Bengali 2014; emphasis added).

The Brookings Institute found similar results, noting that a college education is one of the best investments a student can make, typically bringing them between **15% to 20% increases in income annually.**

Just for a comparison here, in terms of earning extra money every year, if you put your tuition money in your savings account, you'd probably earn only about 1% interest per year, unless, of course, you have a high-yield account. In that case, you'd earn a whopping 2.35%!

What would you rather have: a 15–20% increase in income, or just 1–2.35%?!

If you're feeling a bit left out of this data because you're planning to earn a certificate (rather than a degree), worry not, for certificate earners benefit as well.

The average earnings increase for those who hold certificates is about $2,500 a year more than those who do not earn this credential (Smith). Keep in mind this is additional money earned *every* year. If you work for just 10 years with your credential and you make the average increase, that means you will earn an extra $25,000 more than someone who did not get that credential.

What this research shows is that once you get that new job with that bigger paycheck, you'll have the means to pay off any student loan debt you acquired. Granted, it may take you a few years, but once it is paid off, then all the extra money you earn *every year* after that is pure profit.

Here's the bottom line about this myth:
**Don't let the media hype
scare you out of going to college!**

Getting an education may indeed require that you get a student loan, but not necessarily, and it certainly does not mean you'll be "drowning" in hundreds of thousands of dollars of debt.

Even if it turns out you do indeed need a student loan, don't panic! Any debt you acquire in attaining a college education should be weighed against the benefits you'll enjoy once you earn it. In other words, think of it this way: Even if you feel going to college is going to be a bit expensive, consider, too, what it will cost you if you *don't* go.

MYTH #3: Lots of People are Financially and Professionally Successful Without a College Credential

This myth is what's known in academic circles as "The Millionaire College Dropout Story."

Essentially, the story goes something like this: Since Bill Gates, Steve Jobs, and Mark Zuckerberg did not earn college degrees and yet became billionaires, then that must mean that *no one* needs to go to college to achieve this type of long-lasting, high-level success.

Let's begin with the inaccuracies of the "facts" within this myth.

First, Bill Gates, Mark Zuckerberg, and Steve Jobs are not "lots of people." They are only three people, out of the *seven billion* on the planet.

Plus, they **all** went to college.

Admittedly, they did not *finish* college, but they did go, and Zuckerberg actually had the idea for Facebook while he was a student at Harvard University. If he had never gone to Harvard, it's unlikely he would ever have created Facebook or become a billionaire. Gates went to Harvard as well, and Jobs went to Reed College. These schools are among the most prestigious in the world, and being in such an environment is certainly inspirational, to say the least, and these men's stories actually point to the power of education, not the power of dropping out. (We'll return to this point in a bit.)

The other, and most important, issue with this myth is that statistics simply do not bear it out.

In fact, they show the exact opposite: Very few people achieve financial security and professional success without a college education.

During the recession of 2008, for example, the students who completed their educations reaped the benefits: Over 95 % of the jobs created during the recovery went to them—workers with a college education.

Why?

Since the recession of 2008, low-skilled, blue-collar, and clerical jobs have been replaced by high-skill managerial and professional jobs that require a college education.

This fact may explain why the unemployment rate for people with bachelor's degrees is *less than half* that of those who with only a high school credential[3].

This myth that there are "lots" of people succeeding out in the world without a college credential probably persists because it does contain a tiny kernel of truth.

There are indeed a *few* individuals out there who have managed to achieve incredibly inspiring heights of professional success without graduating from college.

They exist.

That's true.

However, lottery winners exist, too. That doesn't mean we should plan our future based on that existence. Our chances of becoming financially secure without a college credential are only slightly better than winning the Mega Millions lottery.

The people who do mange to buck these odds are **outliers**, meaning they are a rare exception, *not* the norm.

Billionaires like Gates, Jobs, and Zuckerberg achieved immense success without finishing their college educations because they possess some impressive advantages that most of us unfortunately do not have.

These advantages include:

- **The men spent decades developing a set of highly specialized skills** *before* **they arrived at college**
  - Gates and Jobs worked tirelessly for years developing their products and skills, and Zuckerberg attended one of the most elite boarding schools in the world (Exeter), so by the time these men arrived at college, their skillsets exceeded those of the other students, and in some cases, their professors'.
- **All three men had exceptional abilities to educate themselves and received some of the best educations in the world** *before* **college**
  - These men attended some of the best prep schools in the country before attending college, which means they already learned in middle or high school what "regular people" like you and I do not learn until college.
- **They are/were white, middle-class males**
  - It shouldn't matter what their gender, race, or socioeconomic status are in regard to whether they succeeded in their ventures or not, but most of us know these facts sadly do often matter because they convey a set of social, economic, and political privileges these men leveraged to help them succeed.

- **They were already well connected with wealthy, influential people**
  - All three men developed networks of rich and influential family members, friends, and acquaintances who helped open doors for them and provide a safety net in case they failed at their ventures.
  - For example, Zuckerberg received a $500,000 investment from a wealthy backer named Peter Thiel, a man he met through his connections at Harvard. (It must be nice to have such rich friends!)

It's important to understand that outliers like these men did not become successful *because* they dropped out of college.

They became successful *despite* that fact, which is evidenced by the millions and millions of other people who have dropped out of college and did not go on to see that kind of success.

In fact, Gates himself encourages people to go to college. Here's what he said in a 2015 interview:

> College graduates are more likely to find a rewarding job, earn higher income, and even, evidence shows, live healthier lives than if they didn't have degrees... It's just too bad that we're not producing more of them.[4]

Gates is right, too. For those of us without access to the impressive resources he and Jobs and Zuckerberg had, our chances of success without college are, sadly, quite dismal.

In fact, a college credential has become a necessity for economic opportunity.

An estimated two-thirds of job openings now require postsecondary education or training. (For even more data, see the work of Carnevale, Smith, and Strohi 2013).

As workers, we simply cannot ignore these facts in favor of an urban myth.

That's not to say that you shouldn't follow your dreams if they take you above and beyond college. You should. Follow them—by all means!

However, the idea that college will hold you back from those dreams is just not likely to be true. In fact, it's most likely the opposite.

If you want to try a risky business venture, then do it! But, do it later on down the road *after* college because the education you'll receive in your classes will almost certainly *help* you, not hinder you.

Myth #4: You Have to Be Really, Really Smart to Go to College

Intelligence definitely helps in college, but it's not the most important attribute that leads to success. In fact, the most successful college students are not necessarily those who have the most natural intelligence. It's the ones with the most *determination*.

This stick-to-it-ness is referred to in education circles as "grit," a characteristic Dr. Angela Duckworth describes as "passion and perseverance for long-term goals" ("Grit").

To really understand what grit is, Dr. Duckworth suggests we think of it in terms of what it is not: "Grit isn't talent. Grit isn't luck. Grit isn't how intensely, for the moment, you want something. Instead, grit is ... about holding steadfast to your goal. Even when you fall down. Even when you screw up. Even when progress toward that goal is halting or slow" ("Grit.").

Can you immediately see the powerful distinction here between a person with mere "smarts" and one who has grit or determination?

Imagine, for example, two students. The first, Crystal, is one of the smartest students in her class, a genius, even, but she's not necessarily passionate about college. Crystal does not particularly care about persevering in the face of obstacles in her classes because she isn't even sure she wants to be in college.

Now, imagine the second student, Maria, who may not be as intellectually gifted as Crystal, but who has deep, powerful passion about college and is absolutely, 100% determined to become a nurse. It's her life goal, and she won't stop until it becomes her reality.

Who do you think will be more successful in college: Crystal or Maria?

Based on the information we have, I'd bet on Maria—and the research bears this out.

This deep determination or "grit" has been positively associated again and again with successful college outcomes, including grades (Duckworth et al. 2009).

Grit has even been shown to predict several other important qualities:

1. Happiness and life satisfaction (Singh and Jha 2008)
2. Educational success and retention (Duckworth and Quinn 2009)
3. Self-efficacy (Rojas 2015)

How "gritty" a student becomes can also positively predict his/her G.P.A., regardless of the student's age, race, gender, or socioeconomic background! (See Strayhorn 2015 for more information.)

So, if this is all true—that becoming grittier helps you succeed in college, and perhaps in life—how can you achieve it?

How can you become grittier?

Dr. Duckworth suggests developing four core traits:

1. **Interest**
2. **Practice**
3. **Purpose**
4. **Hope**

Interest

Being passionate starts with being interested in what you're doing. People who are gritty find a way to get interested, at least somewhat, in everything that they do.

Granted, this can be difficult to do in classes that aren't exactly your favorites, but if you can cultivate more interest in those classes, it will help you make it to graduation.

For example, if you are given a "boring" topic to write about in your English Composition class, instead of viewing the essay as a chore, try to find a way to get connected with it. If you just can't get interested in the topic itself, then get interested in the *writing* and all the skills that learning to write will bring you (such as strengthening your communication powers, leaning how to organize your thoughts, and defending your ideas, etc.)

Practice

Perseverance isn't necessarily something you're born with—it's something you must practice and develop, so if you feel you're not as good at persevering through challenges as you'd like to be, that's okay. You can get better. You can persevere at persevering!

Try to increase your determination daily by giving yourself goals to reach.

For example, if you struggle to discipline yourself to work on tricky math homework that you hate, force yourself to work on that math for a small amount of time each day, say for 20 minutes on day one—and then reward yourself for your success.

Your brain will slowly start to positively associate the work with the reward, and the discipline will get easier. Then, try to increase that time just a little each day, even if it's only a few minutes more. Keep increasing that time a little bit each day until you make it up to your total needed study time.

Remember that your goal here is simply to practice and get better—*not* to be perfect. Practice won't make you perfect, but it will make you better!

> **Try to do better today than you did yesterday, and remember—you're still learning.**

If you make a mistake, don't be so hard on yourself. Remember that you're *practicing*, and the more you practice, the better you'll get. College isn't about proving how smart you are; it's about *becoming* smarter.

Purpose

Remind yourself often what your "Why" is, your purpose. In other words:

Why are you in college?
Why do you want to get the certificate or degree?

Keeping your "why" in mind will help you to keep your eye on the prize so to speak.

It will help you remember the reason you're doing all this work. When it gets challenging and part of you wants to just give up, those reasons why you *shouldn't* give up will spring up in your mind and heart, and they will inspire you to keep going.

Some students keep an inspiring picture on their phone or hang up inspiring pictures on their walls to remind them of their "why" and to help them envision their goals. For example, one of my students found an image of a face-less college graduate in cap and gown. She downloaded it and then pasted her own face onto it so that *she* was now the smiling graduate. She kept that picture on her phone and looked at it every day.

When she would want to give up on college because of a tough class or instructor, she'd pull out her phone and look at that picture. She'd see her own face smiling up at her with a graduation cap on, reminding her of why she was doing all this work. She would then swallow down her frustration and keep going. Now, she is a college graduate and working in the field of her dreams.

You can do that, too, but you have to remind yourself of your purpose—and do it often.

Hope

People often discount the value of hope, thinking it's a sentiment best left to Sunday morning sermons. Yet, many studies have discovered that developing *hope* actually increases students' graduation rates. (See Figure 2.1 below.)

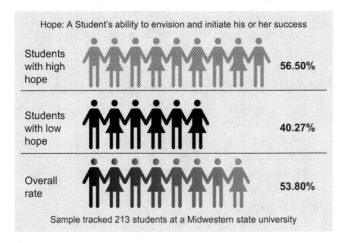

Figure 2.1 Graduation Rates of Students with High Hope vs. Low Hope

How can *you* develop higher levels of hope?

Professors at Santa Clara University suggest giving yourself "hope interventions:"[5]

- Make a list of things you hope for in life and why
- List an obstacle or two that is currently in your way and brainstorm ways to overcome it. If you can't think of any solutions, brainstorm people (advisors, counselors, librarians, professors, fellow students, employers, etc.) or resources (Internet, library, etc.) that you could seek out to help find the answers
- Map out the steps to achieving your goals—be as specific as possible, and reach out to others for help if you're not sure what the steps are or how to complete them
- Write out things that motivate you and brainstorm how you can use these to increase your hope for the future
- Visualize achieving your goals for 30–60 seconds each day

Remember, being smart in college is great, but intelligence alone is *not enough* to succeed.

You must be—and stay—determined.

Don't let your fellow students get you caught up in the race to prove who's the smartest. That doesn't matter, anyway. Just focus on your goals, work hard, and *don't give up*. You will make it eventually, and you'll be so, so glad you did.

Myth #5: Professors Are Mean and Often Embarrass Students in Class—and Enjoy Doing So

The professor's job is to help and support you, and colleges and universities will <u>not</u> allow professors to abuse or emotionally harm students. And, happily, most professors have no interest in doing that, anyway. Professors become professors because they love teaching, and they love helping students.

In fact, getting to know students and helping them is the best part of our jobs.

Your professors have nothing to gain by your failure, but much to gain by your success. They didn't go into teaching because they hate or want to embarrass students. It's the exact opposite: Most professors love their students, love teaching, and love the subject they teach.

Besides, they want to create a classroom of learning and enrichment, and embarrassing students will *not* do that; it will do the exact opposite.

That's not to say you will never encounter a grumpy professor who sees it as his mission in life to "weed out" undesirable students. Sadly, there are a few of these professors out there, but they're the exception, not the rule. Most professors are happy to help students and love doing so.

If you ever do encounter a professor who is rude, disrespectful, or inappropriate with you or another student, report him or her to their department chair and/or your dean immediately. That kind of behavior is unacceptable, and it's important you protect yourself and others from such a predator. Happily, though, you'll find most of your instructors are kind and helpful.

I should say here, though, that you should not equate "kind" with "easy."

Simply because a professor is kind and caring does not mean he or she will *give* you a grade you did not *earn*.

Many students perceive a professor who has high standards as "mean," but that is not an accurate representation.

Your instructors can and should demand a great deal of you. They should not allow you to get away with sloppy, careless work in the interest of being "kind" because, in the long run, these allowances are *not* kind, since they won't prepare you for future coursework or for your future professional life.

Will your boss allow you to "slide" on work because your kids were sick?

Will you win that scholarship if you turn in the application late because you had a doctor's appointment on the due date?

I'm sure you know the answer to these questions is "no."

Therefore, if your professor similarly will not allow you to turn in late work, remember that it is not because they are being "mean" but because they are trying to help you learn to develop professional skills that will serve you later.

As an instructor myself, I can tell you that it is not easy to deliver a high level of rigor and help students become professional and disciplined while also being kind and friendly. So, please cut your professors a bit of slack in this regard, as many of them are still learning how to navigate this complexity. However, don't give them so much slack that you're allowing them to treat you in harmful or unfair ways.

If you're unsure if a professor is behaving inappropriately or not, check for these red flags:

(1) **Lack of equity**

All students should be treated equally and fairly by the professor; if they are not, then we have a problem on our hands.

The instructor should not give more attention to one student than another, regardless of skill level. If you feel the instructor is giving too much time and attention to one particular student or group of students, request a private meeting with him or her and share your concerns in a courteous, respectful way.

If the professor refuses to change, you may have to contact his/her supervisor. Most likely, though, the professor just did not notice and will apologize and fix the problem.

Remember, professors are humans, too, and we make mistakes, so as long as you are respectful about it, what you'll likely receive in return for your feedback is gratitude.

(2) **Failure to listen**

Professors should always be open to listening to their students. If they aren't, then you have a problem and should do your best to let the professor know how you feel. If she simply won't hear you and the problem continues, then you can proceed to her boss (the dean and/or department chair) to get help.

(3) **No open door policy**

All students should be invited to confer with the professor during office hours, and these hours should be posted on the syllabus. If you are not given any office hours, politely request them. If the professor refuses to provide them, you may have to contact the department chair or dean. All students should be able to meet with their professors for help with course material. It's not an option; it's a requirement.

(4) **Name calling**

Under <u>no</u> circumstances whatsoever should a professor call you or any other student names or engage in abuse of any kind. Examples of abuse may include:

- Threats
- Offensive nicknames or bullying
- Name-calling of students (such as "stupid," "idiot," "moron," etc.)
- Sexual, sexist, homophobic, or racist language

If you're not sure if your professor's behavior counts as "abusive" or not, you may want to consult other students and gauge their perceptions. Have they felt uncomfortable, too?

If you determine the behavior is indeed abusive, you can then go to the professor with your concerns and see if you can settle it with him or her.

If he/she apologizes and fixes the behavior, perhaps this is the end of it— that's your choice, depending on the severity.

If the professor does not fix the behavior, however, you will need to speak to his/her supervisor to make sure it does indeed change.

It's important to confront this behavior, not only for yourself but for future students as well, and ultimately for the professor's benefit, too, for if he/she is behaving in this way, something is wrong in his/her life, and those issues need to be handled.

Advisors, deans, and counselors can also help with any issues you encounter with professors.

Having said all that, though, happily you most likely won't encounter any of these problems in your classes, as these occurrences are rarities. Most of your professors will be professional, courteous, and considerate, and hopefully you'll find them among the most inspiring people you've ever met.

Myth #6: College Is Zero Tolerance. One Mistake—and You're Finished!

If this myth were true, no student would ever graduate because *every* student makes mistakes.

Yes, *every* student—even straight-A Honors students. I know because I was a straight-A Honors student. Yet, I made many, many, many mistakes in college. I failed a few tests. I turned in terrible essays, forgot math formulas, and saw the red pen bleed all over essays I thought were fantastic.

And, I'm not alone. Many students experience similar issues. Yet, if we made so many mistakes, how did we succeed? We succeeded not in spite of our mistakes but *because* of them. This point might sound counter-intuitive at first, but it's actually a well-documented phenomena termed in educational research as **productive failure**.

Productive failure is essentially this: Fail first, so you can learn.

By "failing," you will understand what you don't yet understand, and that insight into what you don't yet know will lead you to success—that is, if you learn from the mistake and grow as a result of it.

Psychologist Janet Metcalfe's research nicely illustrates this principle. She studied the outcomes of mistakes for two groups of students:

(1) Students who avoided mistakes at all costs
(2) Students who were okay with mistakes but then sought to correct them

The students who avoided mistakes at all costs performed *worse* on tests than those who didn't fear mistakes but instead worked to correct them (Metcalfe 2017).

So, when you make a mistake in college (and you *will* because we all do!), don't panic, and definitely don't quit.

Mistakes and struggle are part of the process.

Your job is not to avoid them but to *learn* from them. When you do that, you'll become better as a result of them.

We'll discuss this point in further depth in Chapter 8 and go over specific ways that you can do that, but consider now, for example, what you could do if you failed a math test.

There are many steps you could take to turn this "failure" into a learning experience, including:
- Re-working all the problems on the test
  - See if you can figure out the solutions
- Looking at your steps; seeing where you went wrong
  - Highlight those mistakes and re-train your brain to work them out correctly
- Going to office hours or the learning lab
- Examining your study methods, etc., etc.

The key here is to remember that there's no way to be perfect. It's simply not possible, so don't strive for perfection. Instead, strive for improvement—strive to always do and be better than you were yesterday.

Myth #7: You Have to Give Up *Everything* Else in Your Life to Succeed in College

Going to college is certainly not easy, and if you are working, raising kids, and taking care of parents and/or grandparents, it's even more challenging. It might feel so challenging, in fact, that you wonder if you can even succeed at all.

The good news is that you are definitely not alone in this struggle. In the United States today, nearly 14 million people are working and formally enrolled in college[6]. These students did not give up "everything," and neither should you.

If you're wondering if these students can succeed since they are not giving up "everything" to go to college, I have even more good news to share: Georgetown University found that students who complete college degrees *while working* are more likely to transition to managerial positions with higher wages than people who go straight into full-time work after high school (Carnevale 2015).

Yes, you read that correctly:

> The fact that you are working and going to school at the same time is a strong predictor of your future success!

If you think about this fact for a few minutes, you'll easily see why it's true.

Although your struggles are certainly challenging, they are also highly beneficial because:

- You're learning to balance your time
- You're learning to handle high stress and pressure
- You're expanding your abilities, increasing your knowledge, and sharpening your skillset
- You're learning to make a commitment, even when in a challenging environment

These are highly sought-after skills that employers greatly value—and they're skills that will help you in many areas of your life, above and beyond college and work.

However, if you feel you're not quite excelling in this area of achieving balance, don't worry. You'll get better as you practice throughout your college career, and in Chapter 7 we'll cover specific ways you can begin to develop this ability further —and rest assured you do *not* have to give up everything in your life outside of school to succeed.

Your fellow adult students all over the country are learning to achieve this balance in their work, home, and school lives, and you will, too.

Myth # 8: In College, You're on Your Own; No One Will Help You

Every college and university employs teams of people hired solely to help you succeed. In fact, everyone working at your college—your professors, advisors, tutors, librarians, counselors, and even the president—is invested in your success.

Here's why: **When you succeed, they succeed, too.**

The more successful an institution's graduates are, the more successful the institution is.

The only catch here is that you, as the student, must do your part and reach out for help when you need it—and remember, you *will* need help at some point. We all do, at one time or another, but it's on you to take that step of asking for assistance when you need it.

Some colleges make it very easy to seek help, and others aren't quite as good at advertising the help available to students. So, you may have to do a bit of digging to find the help you need, but even if that turns out to be true, in a way that's good news because you're developing your research skills!

We'll discuss asking for help in greater depth in Chapter 12, but for now, just know that there are help teams available, ready and waiting to assist you. Here's a quick glance at some of the help you can find on your college campus.

Issue	Get Help Here
Holds on student account	Advisers, Counselors, and/or Dean of Students
Problems with financial aid	Financial Aid Office, Adviser, Counselor
Trouble with studying or understanding class material	Professor or TA's Office Hours, Learning Lab (tutoring), or Writing Center, see if your college offers "Academic Coaching" (many do—for free!)
Can't pay for tuition and/or books	Student Emergency Assistance Fund, Textbook Loan Program, Library, Dean of Students, and/or Financial Aid Office

Myth # 9: College Is a Competition; It's Me Against the Other Students

Many students have heard nightmare stories about how college is like the old television program *Survivor*, where contestants try to beat each other out to win a prize and avoid being voted off the "island."

I have good news in this vein: College is nothing like *Survivor*.

You're not competing with the other students for any prize, and there's no "voting off the island," so don't imagine college in that way.

Although it is true that occasionally instructors will give out only so many "A"s or "B"s in a class, this is a rare practice, and besides, making friends with the other students is much more likely to *help* your grade than to hurt it.

This is an important point, so let me repeat it:

Becoming friends with your fellow students will almost certainly *help* your grades.

How, you ask?

Forming friendships with your fellow students offers you many benefits:

- Joining **study groups** can increase your understanding of course material
- Gaining access to **another student's resources,** such as their notes, books, etc. gives you increased perspective on course materials
- Getting **another set of eyes on your work** means free feedback to help you improve (this is especially important in classes that require writing)
- **Discussing ideas** presented in class or for developing your own work expands your understanding of an audience's perception of your viewpoint
- **Celebrating victories** on tests, quizzes, etc. boosts your confidence
- **Having an ally** in class with whom you can commiserate leads to a more positive experience

In addition to these benefits, forming friendships with your classmates will help you to increase your ability to work and get along with others, a skill highly valued by employers.

So, remember: Your fellow students are your *friends*, not at all your enemies, so don't see them that way.

If your relationships with other students in class will distract you from learning, then by all means do what is best for you. However, usually, your fellow students are a resource and a source of help and inspiration. When you don't understand something, consider asking one of them. Perhaps they can explain it in a new way that will help you understand it better.

Remember, too, that friendship is a two-way street, so be sure to offer *your* help to other students, too. If your neighbor looks confused and you're not, ask if you can help.

Remember:
Your fellow students can help you, and you can help them.
They are your friends, NOT your competition.

Besides, you never know when you might just need *their* help, so do your best to make friends with your fellow students, whenever and wherever you can...

Myth #10: Most College Students Know *Exactly* What They Want to Do With Their Lives

Many students may enter college *thinking* they know what they want to do with their lives, but in actuality, a sizable percentage of students change their minds. Check out this data from the U.S. Department of Education[7] on students switching majors:

- 52% of math majors switched
- 40% of natural sciences majors switched
- 37% of education majors switched
- 36% of humanities majors switched
- 35% of all STEM majors switched
- 32% of engineering majors switched
- 32% of general studies majors switched
- 31% of social science majors switched
- 31% of business majors switched
- 28% of computer and information sciences majors switched
- 26% of healthcare field majors switched

Like these students, chances are good that you may change your major, too—and it's perfectly okay. In fact, many people (including myself) would argue that ideally going to college is about exploration and discovery, and this exploration and discovery include figuring out your major.

Granted, some schools will strongly discourage you from changing your major because it might delay your graduation date, and this delay may count against the school's "success" numbers. Yet, a 2016 study suggests that students who change their major graduate at slightly higher rates than those who don't. (See the chart in Figure 2.2 for more information.)

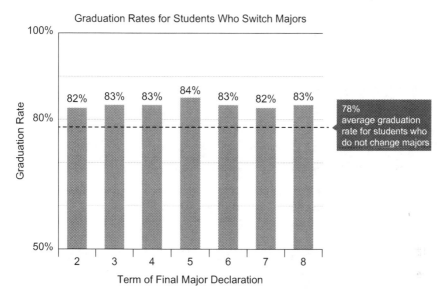

Figure 2.2 Graduation Rates for Students Who Switch Majors

This data suggests switching majors can be a *positive experience* for some students because it allows them the opportunity to explore and discover, to find a major about which they are very passionate.

There are so many different careers and majors available that it is unlikely a new college student can know about *all* of them, so the opportunity to attend different classes and learn more about the potential jobs they can do helps them make a more informed decision (thus the change in major).

As an adult student, you are probably in a hurry and on a limited budget when it comes to college. So, you probably don't want to change your major *too* many times. However, you also don't want to stick with a bad choice, either, so if you do change your mind on your major as you proceed through your classes, know that it's okay. Students often change their majors as they respond to their own changing interests during their college experience, and your willingness to do so is actually a sign of wisdom and maturity.

You Have Options

Some universities and colleges, such as Georgetown State University, allow students to choose what they call "**metamajors**," which are clusters of courses in the same general field, such as business, humanities, or STEM, for example. These majors allow undeclared students to discover areas of interest while at the same time giving them a somewhat structured pathway toward graduation.

If you're interested in this type of major, inquire at your college or university to see if they offer something similar to the metamajor. If not, inquire what other options are available to you. Most schools are happy to work with their students to ensure they are content and successful.

"Wasted" Classes

Many students worry about changing majors because they fear they will end up "wasting" the classes they've already taken. Don't worry about "wasting" classes because it's simply not possible. Any classes that you take give you wisdom and knowledge and experience, so the time and money invested in them is *never* wasted. They've made you stronger and smarter, so instead of wasting time worrying about them, re-invest that energy into choosing the best major and degree or certificate for you. (We'll discuss this topic in greater depth in Chapter 3).

SUGGESTED EXERCISE:

Re-take the College Myth Quiz below (rephrased and made a bit more difficult!) to see if you truly understand myths versus truths about college life. The answer key is in small type below.

1. **True/False.** Researchers at Dartmouth University concluded that the adult brain is not as capable of learning and expanding as younger brains are.
2. **True/False.** Only wealthy students can go to college without taking out loans.
3. **True/False.** Most college students today are "non-traditional students," meaning they are over 25 years of age, have children, work at least part-time, or are veterans.
4. **True/False.** While it's possible to be financially and professionally successful without a college credential, statistically speaking, it's not likely.
5. **True/False.** Researchers discovered that developing *hope* actually increases students' graduation rates.
6. **True/False.** *All* college students make mistakes and need help from time to time.
7. **True/False.** Colleges and universities employ teams of hundreds, possibly thousands, of people whose primary job is to help students succeed.
8. **True/False.** Making friends with your fellow students is almost certain to help your grades.

9. **True/False.** About 80% of college students change their major at least once.
10. **True/False.** At some colleges, students who are uncertain of their major are allowed to major in what's called "metamajors," which are clusters of courses in the same general field (such as business, humanities, or STEM). These majors allow undeclared students to discover areas of interest while still having a somewhat structured pathway toward graduation.

Answer Key:

1. F, 2. F, 3. T, 4. T, 5. T, 6. T, 7. T, 8. T, 9. T, 10. T

Notes

1 Read the full article here: https://psychologytoday.com/blog/canine-corner/201602/you-can-teach-old-dog-new-tricks
2 Read the full report here: https://cew.georgetown.edu/cew-reports/the-college-payoff/
3 Read the full article here: https://.bls.gov/opub/ted/2018/unemployment-rate-2-1-percent-for-college-grads-3-9-percent-for-high-school-grads-in-august-2018.htm?view_full.
4 Read his full statement here: https://gatesnotes.com/Education/11-Million-College-Grads
5 Read the full article by Feldman and Dreher here: https://link.springer.com/article/10.1007/s10902-011-9292-4
6 Read the full article by Carnevale (et al.) here: https://cew.georgetown.edu/wp-content/uploads/Working-Learners-Report.pdf
7 Read the full report here: https://nces.ed.gov/pubs2018/2018434.pdf

3 Choose the Best Major and Degree or Certificate for You

IN THIS CHAPTER, YOU WILL LEARN:

- How to select your major
- The primary differences between degrees and certificates (and the pros and cons of both)
- How to choose the best degree or certificate plan for you

Most of the adult students I've met and worked with over the last decade and a half share one thing in common: They're in a hurry!

They feel like they're behind when it comes to getting an education, so they want to make up for that lost time by rushing through college. So, when choosing a major, they pick the quickest option available to them and try to rush through the requirements of the degree or certificate as speedily as possible.

The problem with this approach is that it is short-sighted, for it asks you to sacrifice your future working life so you can "get through" college quickly.

I understand that there are bills to pay and kids to raise and jobs to get, but that will always be true. It's better to take your time and pick the right major and degree or certificate for you than it is to rush to pick something that's just "ok" so you can hurry up and be done.

Remember, whatever job you get with your college credential will probably require you to work eight hours per day, five days per week for years and years and years, possibly for *decades*. That means you'll spend more than half of your waking life at this job—for possibly the next decade or two. So, in light of this fact, I recommend you make this choice based on *wisdom*, not haste.

After all, why did you come back to school if not to get a better, more satisfying career that you'll actually enjoy? You can get a stressful job you don't like with a high school credential. Granted, you'll earn more money with a college credential than you will with just a high school one, but isn't your overall satisfaction in life worth something, too?

Additionally, think of the impact of your choices on those around you. Will you, for example, be able to be a good parent, wife, husband, daughter, son, or community member, etc. if you're constantly stressed over a job that you rushed to get but don't really like?

I know it's hard not to be in a hurry, but just remember why you're here—to get a better career, and a better life overall. If you're going to go to all the stress and effort and cost to go to college, isn't it better to take your time and do it right?

Make sure you do just that by asking yourself this question: **Do you want to earn a certificate or degree—or perhaps both—and why?**

Many students aren't sure, exactly, what the differences are between the two, so let's go over both, and then we'll also cover the pros and cons of each.

There are essentially three key differences between a "degree" and a "certificate":

1. **Number of credit hours** (and thus time) needed to earn
2. **Transferability** of the classes
3. **Type and quality of work** you can get by earning

Read the chart on the following page for more information detailing these differences.

Certificate Versus Degree

Certificate	*Degree*
• Takes about a year to earn	• Takes at least two years to earn, depending on which degree you seek
	Associate's Degree = 2–3 years **Bachelor's Degree** = 4–5 years (total) **Master's Degree** = 6–7 years (total) **Medical or PhD** = 8–12 years (total)
• Classes focus solely on the *field/major*, not on general studies. • It will likely *not* require you to take English, history, math, literature, science, etc.	• Classes are taken from many fields to produce a well-rounded, highly knowledgeable person • Usually requires taking English, history, math, literature, science, etc.

(Continued)

(*Continued*)

Certificate	Degree
• Usually about 25–30 credit hours • (A "credit hour" is the number of credits you earn per course. See Appendix A for a complete definition and examples)	• **Associate's Degree = 60 credit hours** • **Bachelor's Degree = 120 credit hours** (If you have an Associate's, you can subtract those 60 hours from the 120 total here, so you'd probably only need about 60 hours *more* to get the Bachelor's. See Appendix D for more information on transferring credits.) • **Master's Degree** = *another* 30 hours (on top of the 120 for the Bachelor's) • **Law, Medical, or PhD** = Depends on field; usually requires lengthy residency or internship hours (typically *another* 3–7 years above the Bachelor's)
• Classes **usually do *not* transfer**, meaning that if you want to continue your education to get a degree, the hours earned in certificate classes **may not count toward the degree**	• As long as you attend an accredited institution, your class hours will likely transfer. (For more information on transferring your credit hours to another school, see Appendix D and for more on accreditation, see Chapter 6)

Which one is best for you: certificate or degree (or both)? To find out, let's go over the pros and cons of each.

Pros and Cons

	Pros	Cons
Certificate	• **Quick**—usually only takes about a year to earn • Gives you **hands-on experience** in your field • Can lead to work *immediately* • Can be an amazing confidence builder because it's a *completion* of college credit and a great way to get your feet wet in college, so to speak	• Whether you can actually get work with it depends. Some certificates are valuable; some aren't. • Talk to practitioners and other workforce experts in your field BEFORE you take certificate classes. Ensure the certificate you want is considered valuable in the field. • Classes often don't transfer to a university, and many don't count toward the degree

(*Continued*)

(*Continued*)

	Pros	Cons
Degree	• More prestigious than certificate, and often more highly valued by employers (but this depends on the degree and the employer) • Usually leads to higher paying, more stable and long-term work than the certificate • Helps you become more well-rounded and grounds you in a firm understanding of many aspects of our complicated, complex society • Develops strong critical thinking and analytical skills	• Takes years to earn • Is more expensive • Requires you to take classes outside your major that you may not like (literature, science, math, etc.) • May not offer hands-on experience or training, although some do. (Check with your advisor or dean.) • Not all degrees are created equal. Some are almost instantly high-earning (such as computer science or engineering). Others (such as English, psychology, or communications) may take years to lead to high-paying, stable work.

The good news here is that both degrees and certificates are valuable; it's just a matter of what you—and your future employers—prize.

For this reason, consider yet another option here: Earn *both* a certificate *and* a degree and acquire stackable credentials.

Stackable Credentials

Many people start with earning a certificate first and then later add a degree or two. Still other people do the opposite: They earn a degree first, and then add a certificate later to make themselves more marketable.

This strategy of earning credentials slowly over time and building on them is called earning **stackable credentials**—meaning that you first earn one credential, and then you stack another on top of it.

For example, you could first earn a certificate in nursing (say, a CNA). Then, you could use that CNA to get a job working in the field and gaining valuable experience. (This experience would also tell you if you actually enjoy the work you're doing!) Then, as you're establishing yourself as a CNA, you could proceed toward working on your Associate's Degree in Nursing (ADN). Once you earn that credential and pass the Registered Nurse (RN) exam, you could gain work as a Registered Nurse. If you so choose, you could then work toward a Bachelor's, or even a Master's Degree in Nursing, to earn further promotions and gain even more extensive knowledge in your field.

These stackable credentials can work well in many fields, so if you're interested, check with your advisor, Career Center, and/or people working in the field to see if this strategy works well in that particular profession.

CAUTION: Be sure that you check data in the actual field before you pursue this strategy. Unfortunately, there are a few certificates offered by colleges that do **not** lead to jobs in the field, so always double, even triple, check to make sure the one(s) you want will actually lead to the type of work you seek.

Certificate or Degree: Which is Best For You?

Now that you understand the differences between certificates and degrees a bit better, you're probably wondering which is best for you. If you're still not sure, try these steps to help you figure it out:

1. **Study job advertisements for the type of job(s) you want to get after college**
   - See what level of education is required, or even preferred. Do employers seek a certificate, or do they want candidates only with a degree? In what major(s)?
   - Check multiple sources—local newspapers, LinkedIn.Com, Indeed. Com, Monster.Com, etc.
2. **Talk to people who work in the field**
   - Reach out to others working in the field and ask them what education or training is required to get the job you seek
   - Get on LinkedIn and request connection with people working in the field. Then, look at their credentials and education to see what certificate or degree they earned and ask them for recommendations and advice about how to find work in the field
   - Ask your professors, advisors, and department chairs for recommendations, or just get online to research for yourself
3. **If your college has career advisors, make an appointment**
   - Most colleges offer career services, so take advantage and book an appointment
   - Write out your questions in advance so you can maximize your appointment time
4. **If your city/area has a Workforce Help Center, visit it**
   - These services are funded by your tax dollars, so take advantage and book an appointment!
   - These career advisors spend all day every day researching what fields are the hottest in your area, so ask them what they recommend and how you can get work in these fields
   - These Centers probably also offer free computer access and even job search services and classes, so inquire about what help is available

Suggested Degree and Certificate Plans

Below, we'll go over some suggestions for potential degrees and certificates you might want to consider, but keep in mind these are just suggestions.

You'll want to do your own research as well to see what careers are "hot" in your area or of the most interest to you.

We'll start with potential degrees to earn, and then we'll proceed to prospective certificates.

Potential Degrees to Earn

Since most students are at least partially motivated by the income they'll earn from their future occupation, you will find on the following page the highest-paying occupations by education, including the job prospects for these occupations, according to the U.S. Department of Labor.[1]

Remember, though, that your paycheck is only *one* aspect of your job, and you should ask yourself what exactly is most important to *you* about your future career.

In other words, what do you care *most* about in your future work?

- The rewarding nature of the work?
- The flexible hours?
- Working with people?
- Getting to perform different, unique tasks every day?

Think carefully about these questions and then make your decision based on what **you** feel are your most important future occupation's characteristics.

You may also want to ask the questions below, too:

What type of work would best suit you?

- What do you most like to do?
- What are your skills?
- What are your talents and strengths?
- What motivates you to work the hardest?
- What type of work will leave you feeling satisfied and happy?
- What jobs fit well with your personality?
- What are your core values, and how could those values relate to or inform your career choice?

Associate's Degree Potential Majors and Occupations: Figure 3.1

Please note that the data in Figure 3.1 displays *national* data. You'll want to check the data in your local and/or state area to make sure the occupation you choose is in demand where you live (unless, of course, you're willing to move!).

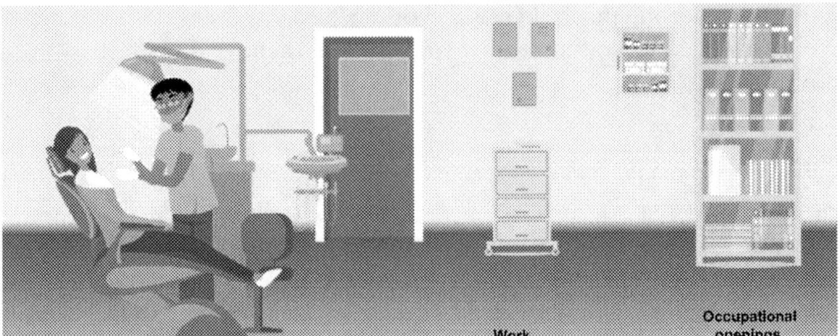

Occupation	Median annual wage, 2017 [1]	Work experience in a related occupation	On-the-job training	Occupational openings, projected 2016–26 annual average
Air traffic controllers	$124,540	None	Long term	2,400
Radiation therapists	80,570	None	None	1,200
Nuclear technicians	80,370	None	Moderate term	800
Funeral service managers	78,040	Less than 5 years	None	2,000
Nuclear medicine technologists	75,660	None	None	1,300
Dental hygienists	74,070	None	None	17,500
Diagnostic medical sonographers	71,410	None	None	5,400

[1] Data exclude wages of self-employed workers.
Source: U.S. Bureau of Labor Statistics, Office of Occupational Statistics and Employment Projections.

Figure 3.1 Highest-Paying Occupations for Associate's Degrees

Potential Certificates to Earn

You'll find in Figure 3.2 the top ten certificate programs that lead to high-paying jobs and fulfilling careers (according to the Department of Labor).

Non-Degree Potential Majors and Occupations: Figure 3.2

Again, keep in mind that this data is *national* in scope, so it may or may not be a good fit for your area. You can and should also check with your college's career center or visit a Workforce Center in your area to discover what certificates are in demand where you live (unless, of course, you don't mind moving!).

Choosing a Major

Once you've decided on your degree or certificate, this choice might just decide your major for you as well, but not necessarily. If, for example, you

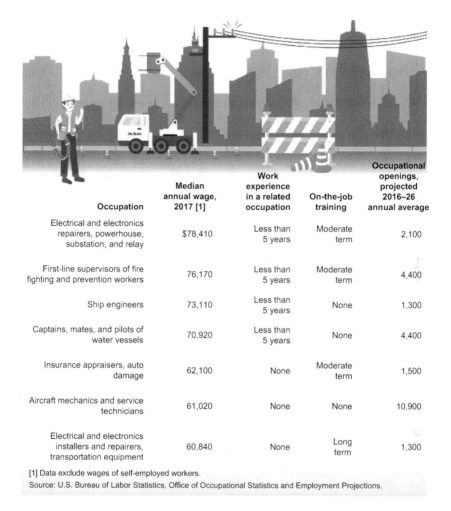

Occupation	Median annual wage, 2017 [1]	Work experience in a related occupation	On-the-job training	Occupational openings, projected 2016–26 annual average
Electrical and electronics repairers, powerhouse, substation, and relay	$78,410	Less than 5 years	Moderate term	2,100
First-line supervisors of fire fighting and prevention workers	76,170	Less than 5 years	Moderate term	4,400
Ship engineers	73,110	Less than 5 years	None	1,300
Captains, mates, and pilots of water vessels	70,920	Less than 5 years	None	4,400
Insurance appraisers, auto damage	62,100	None	Moderate term	1,500
Aircraft mechanics and service technicians	61,020	None	None	10,900
Electrical and electronics installers and repairers, transportation equipment	60,840	None	Long term	1,300

[1] Data exclude wages of self-employed workers.

Source: U.S. Bureau of Labor Statistics, Office of Occupational Statistics and Employment Projections.

Figure 3.2 Highest-Paying Occupations for Certificate Holders

already know you want to go into the field of Criminal Justice, then you may assume your major will be Criminal Justice. Not so fast. What, exactly, do you want to do within that field?

Do you want to be a crime scene investigator? A paralegal? A criminal attorney?

If you decided to go the path of crime scene investigator, then the criminal justice major is probably a good idea. However, if you want to be an attorney, a major in history, psychology, or government might be better choices (with perhaps a minor in criminal justice). Or, conversely, perhaps you could earn an Associate's degree in criminal justice first to secure work in the field. Then, as you're working in the field and learning, you can go back to school to earn your Bachelor's and eventually law degrees. By the time you graduate law school, you'll be highly, highly knowledgeable in your field!

If you have no idea what you want to major in, don't worry.

It takes time and patience to choose a major, and although I know you probably feel rushed, do your best to slow down and make the right choice, rather than a quick one.

Let's go over some steps below to help you find that major.

Step 1: Take "What's Your Major?" Quizzes

Just as you can take a career aptitude assessment test, you can also take a "What's Your Major?" quiz to help you identify potential majors.

Most colleges now offer these quizzes via their website, so take as many of these as you can. Make a list of the results or print them out and keep them in a special folder or binder. Then, once you feel you've taken enough quizzes, sit down with the data and read through it.

Which major speaks to you?

Which one won't leave you alone and seems to call to you?

That one is your major.

Think, too, about the day-to-day work required in this occupation and whether you would enjoy doing those things. What are the working conditions like? What is the level of human interaction? Is there strong income potential? How much boring, tedious paperwork is involved in the job?

It's crucial you have a full picture of your chosen career before spending years of work and thousands of dollars on a degree. I've sadly met students who spent years earning a credential only to discover they hate doing the actual day-to-day work of the job they worked so hard to get. Although it sounded good on paper, once they got the job, the student discovered it's just not something they want to do. So, now, they're back at square one. Don't let this happen to you! Be sure you know what you're getting into jobwise before you devote so much time, energy, and money to earning a credential to do it. Even if it pays well, the question remains: Will you *enjoy* doing it overall?

Step 2: Listen

There's a saying in higher education, one that many people (myself included) ardently believe in with regard to choosing a major. You may not believe it, and that's perfectly okay because it's undoubtedly an opinion, but it's one that is so powerful I feel I must share it with you, and it is this: *You don't pick your major; your major picks you.*

What does that mean?

It means that if you can calm your fears and reservations and doubts for a few minutes, you'll hear your major calling to you. Listen. It's there. Then, answer the call.

If that advice is too intangible for you, keep trying the more concrete steps below.

Step 3: Step Out and Find Out

Make a list of three to four potential majors, and then **take a course in each** of them. By doing this, you'll get to sample the subject matter and learn more about it. Once you've taken a full course in a certain subject, you'll have a better idea of whether you enjoy doing it, and if you have a strong aptitude for it.

You'll also meet like-minded people (like the professor and other students) who can offer you unique perspectives on the work, so ask them questions and solicit their feedback. Learn as much as you can so that you're making an informed decision based on solid information, not urban myth or speculation.

Step 4: Visit Open Houses

Many departments offer what they call "open houses," meaning they host an informative event on the majors within that department. Faculty and students will be on hand, along with printed information and suggested further resources. Check out these events when offered, and if your prospective majors aren't offering one, find out who is in charge of that department and call or email them to ask if they might consider holding one. Even if they say "no," they might just offer to meet with you in person instead, and if they don't offer, suggest that meeting yourself. If they're saying "no" to your open house request, they probably will not also say no to a meeting request! And, even if they do, at least you did your best.

Step 5: Visit Each of Your Potential Major's Departmental Websites

These sites often have a plethora of information that can help answer your questions about class schedules, course requirements, job opportunities, scholarships, internships, income potential, and day-to-day job duties, etc. Check these sites often, as they are probably updated quarterly and often advertise events, or even jobs, of interest.

Step 6: Schedule a Meeting with the Departmental Representative

Each major most likely has what they call a "departmental representative," which is a person assigned to answer prospective students' questions about the major. Check each of your potential major's websites to see if they have one of these representatives. If not, try emailing or calling the Department

Chair or Dean and asking him/her questions about the major, including job prospects, required coursework, etc. If you have enough questions, they might just grant you an in-person meeting, and if that is the case, you just made your first potential new connection in the field!

Step 7: Look into Internships in Your Potential Majors

Often, colleges offer these non-paying positions exclusively to students. Although they often don't offer financial payment, these internships do offer much in non-monetary benefits, such as experience, contacts, and knowledge.

Step 8: Do Volunteer Work in your Potential Field(s)

Most fields are desperate for dedicated, hardworking volunteers, and often you don't have to make a huge time commitment, either. Many programs will let you commit to as little as one hour per month, so see if you can find a place that can work with your schedule and involves work you might be interested in doing as a career. You'll meet potential mentors here and also gain valuable experience and knowledge.

Step 9: Consider Declaring a Generic Major such as "General Studies"

If you absolutely cannot decide on a major but your college or university requires you to declare one, you can try what many students do: They declare "general studies" to essentially postpone the decision. This way, you can begin your first-year coursework, and hopefully as you proceed through the different courses, you'll begin to see which classes are well suited to you, and which are not—and this almost always helps you make the decision.

I know it's easier said than done, but try not to worry too much about choosing that major. Other well-meaning people will probably try to pressure you into making a choice, but don't let them. The decision is *yours,* so don't let parents, kids, spouses, friends, or family members' ideas of what you *should* be doing determine your future.

You'll make the best decision not under pressure but under peace, so try to be calm and collected, not stressed and frantic.

Step 10: Interview and/or Job Shadow

Find some people currently working in the occupation you would like to pursue. Ask them, or better yet, shadow them to see for yourself: What is an actual day, week, or even month on the job like?

Here is a list of helpful job shadowing and/or interview questions for you to ask, courtesy of Marquette University Career Services Center[2]. These are just suggestions, though, so feel free to add your own questions as well.

1. What are the duties/functions/responsibilities of your job?
2. Is there flexibility related to dress, work hours, vacation schedule, place of residence, etc.?
3. If your job progresses as you like, what would be the next step in your career?
4. With the information you have about my education, skills, and experience, what other fields or jobs would you suggest I research further before I make a final decision?
5. Are there other things you are expected to do outside work hours?
6. What is a typical career path in this field or organization?
7. What is the best way to enter this occupation?
8. How well did your college experience prepare you for this job?
9. What abilities or personal qualities do you believe contribute most to success in this field/job?
10. Do you have any advice for someone interested in this field/job? Are there any written materials you suggest?

Majors Can Always Be Changed

One last note here: You can always change your major.

Granted, a class or two that you took might not count toward the new major, but it's better to simply lose a few credits than to spend years earning a degree in a field you don't really want to enter.

If you're still not certain what your major or career destination is, take a career assessment test, such as MAPP, O*NET, or FOCUS2. You can also check with your college to see if they offer career assessment inventories, and do your own research, too. There are literally thousands of resources you can peruse, both online and in print (see below for suggestions).

SUGGESTED FURTHER RESOURCES

Online Career Assessments:

- https://mbtionline.com/
- https://princetonreview.com/quiz/career-quiz
- https://myplan.com/
- https://profile.keirsey.com/#/b2c/assessment/start
- https://assessment.com/
- https://mynextmove.org/explore/ip
- https://pymetrics.com/employers/

BOOKS:

- *What Color is Your Parachute? A Practical Manual for Job-Hunters and Career-Changers* by Richard N. Bolles
- *Knock 'Em Dead: The Ultimate Job Search Guide* by Martin Yate
- *Do What You Are: Discover the Perfect Career for You Through the Secrets of Personality Type* by Paul D. Tieger and Barbara Barron
- *How to Find Fulfilling Work* by Roman Krznaric
- *I Could Do Anything If I Only Knew What It Was* by Barbara Sher with Barbara Smith
- *The Pathfinder: How to Choose or Change Your Career for a Lifetime of Satisfaction and Success* by Nicholas Lore

JOB RESEARCH SITES:

- www.bls.gov/oco
- https://asaecenter.org/
- http://jobstar.org/

Suggested Exercise:

1) Choose two to three of the online assessments listed on the page above and take them. Write a brief summary of your understanding of the results.
2) Go to the bookstore or library and get a couple of the books listed above. Write a brief summary of what you learned from the book(s) and apply it to your life.
3) Make a list of three to five potential careers and then research them carefully, either using the suggested websites above, or by finding your own sources.

Notes

1 See the full report (by Elka Torpey) here: https://bls.gov/careeroutlook/2019/article/high-wage-occupations.htm
2 See the full list here: https://cals.vt.edu/content/dam/cals_vt_edu/alumni/mentoring/Job-Shadowing-Questions.pdf

4 Find Funds to Pay for Your College Education

IN THIS CHAPTER, YOU WILL LEARN:

- What financial aid is, who qualifies for it, and how **you** can apply for it
- The differences between scholarships, loans, and grants
- What scam schools and diploma mills are—and how to avoid them
- How to spot scholarship and loan scams—and avoid them
- Insider tips on how to get your books and supplies for less—perhaps even for free

---

"Can I afford a college education?"

This is a question most students find themselves asking. Indeed, having enough money to pay for college is probably one of the biggest concerns for most students. Yet, the good news is that there are many resources available to help you pay for college, so don't let money woes stop you from acquiring the level of education that you truly want.

It will most likely take a bit of leg work and research on your part to find these funding sources, but this work is well worth the effort, and happily I've done a great deal of the research for you. Your job will simply be to go through the information, find the sources that are best for you, and apply!

Before we jump into applying, however, let's begin with some definitions to ensure that you understand the different types of financial aid, where you can find them, and how to determine if potential sources are legitimate or scams.

Let's begin with the term "financial aid" itself.

What *is* financial aid, exactly?

Financial aid is monetary assistance that covers educational expenses, such as tuition, fees, books, supplies, and even room and board. This aid can come in several forms:

1. Grants
2. Loans
3. Scholarships
4. Work-study
   (We'll cover each in more depth below.)

What are the sources of financial aid?

The most prominent source of financial aid is the U.S. federal government. It offers aid to qualifying students each year to help them earn a certificate or degree. However, if you do not qualify for federal aid, do not despair! There are other sources of financial aid, too, including:

1. City and state governments
2. Educational institutions (high schools, colleges, universities, etc.)
3. Private businesses and agencies
4. Work-study programs

Who qualifies for financial aid?

Each financial aid source has its own rules and regulations, so check each source's requirements.

Since most students want to qualify for federal financial aid assistance, we'll go over the basic eligibility requirements. To qualify for federal aid, *everyone* must meet these basic requirements (see below). However, please note additional eligibility requirements apply for certain situations. If you aren't sure, check with the financial aid office at your college or university.

Basic Eligibility Criteria for Federal Financial Aid[1]

TO QUALIFY FOR FEDERAL FINANCIAL AID, YOU MUST:

- Demonstrate financial need (for most programs)
- Be a U.S. citizen or an eligible noncitizen
- Have a valid Social Security number (with the exception of students from the Republic of the Marshall Islands, Federated States of Micronesia, or the Republic of Palau)

- Be registered with Selective Service if you're a male (you **must** register between the ages of 18 and 25)
- Be enrolled or accepted for enrollment as a regular student in an eligible degree or certificate program
- Be enrolled at least half-time to be eligible for Direct Loan Program funds
- Maintain satisfactory academic progress in college or career school
- Sign the certification statement on the *Free Application for Federal Student Aid* (F.A.F.S.A.®) stating that:
  - You are not in default on a federal student loan and do not owe money on a federal student grant, and
  - You will use federal student aid only for educational purposes; and
- Show you're qualified to obtain a college or career school education by:
  - Having a high school diploma or a recognized equivalent such as a General Educational Development (GED) certificate;
    Completing a high school education in a homeschool setting approved under state law (or—if state law does not require a homeschooled student to obtain a completion credential— completing a high school education in a homeschool setting that qualifies as an exemption from compulsory attendance requirements under state law); or
  - Enrolling in an eligible career pathway program and meeting one of the "ability-to-benefit" alternatives described below.

If you are male, you also most likely **must** register for "Selective Service" between the ages of 18 and 25 to qualify for federal student aid. (There are a few notable exceptions, though, so if you have not yet registered and are over age 25, check with your adviser and/or financial aid office to inquire about receiving assistance.)

Types of Financial Aid

Grants

Grants are the most popular form of financial aid, one that many students call "free money" because they've heard that you don't have to pay them back—but please note that's not entirely true. Grants have requirements that their recipients **must** meet, so if the student does *not* meet these requirements, then the student usually must pay back the money.

The most popular grants are those offered by the U.S. Department of Education (ED), which offers several types of grants to students:

- Federal Pell Grants
- Federal Supplemental Educational Opportunity Grants (FSEOG)
- Teacher Education Assistance for College and Higher Education (TEACH) Grants
- Iraq and Afghanistan Service Grants

The Federal Pell Grant is the most common grant, so we'll go over this one in detail.

(For more information on the other grants, visit https://studentaid.ed.gov /sa/types/grants-scholarships.)

The Pell is a grant that students can apply for and win each year. The amount awarded currently stands at $6,195 per year, but this amount fluctuates from year to year, so be sure to check for the most updated amount.

To earn—and keep—the money, recipients must follow these rules:

FINANCIAL AID RECIPIENT RULES

1. You must stay enrolled in your classes
2. If you drop some of your classes, you'll likely have to give back that portion of the money
3. If you drop **all** of your classes, you'll have to give back **all** of the money
4. You must enroll in at least six hours of classes (two to three classes)
5. You must make Satisfactory Academic Progress
6. You must re-apply each year that you wish to receive aid

Let's go over each of these rules one by one to ensure understanding.

Rule 1: You must stay enrolled in your classes

Federal grant money comes from U.S. tax dollars, which essentially means that taxpayers are paying you to be a student. Before receiving any money, you'll sign an agreement certifying that you will use federal student aid *only* for educational purposes.

If you're not using the money for these purposes, then you are in violation of the agreement, which means you must pay the money back.

Sadly, there are always a few students who misunderstand these financial aid rules. They hear "free money from the government," and they sign up for classes, then drop them like hot potatoes as soon as the money drops into their bank account. Thinking they're geniuses "beating the system," they go out and buy a new computer, new clothes, and a Playstation, etc.

Sadly, I've known a few students who made this mistake when they were young. Then, when they tried to return to college years later, they were in for an unpleasant surprise: They could not receive any financial aid until they paid back the grant money they received prior. (Also, know that the government can, in severe cases, get a court order to garnish wages to recover student aid money!)

Rule 2: If you drop just a few of your classes, then you have to give back that portion of the money

Consider, for example, a student, Maria, who plans to enroll in four classes in both fall and spring semesters. Maria gets the full financial aid award of $6,195. She accepts the money, but in both semesters, she drops two of her four classes and does not re-enroll in any other classes.

By summer semester, Maria will probably be required to pay back approximately half ($3,000) for the two classes she dropped, or make up those classes in summer.

For this reason, it's probably a good idea to **hold back some of your financial aid money each semester,** if you can, just in case you need to drop a class. (And, yes, you most likely will need to drop one at some point!)

How much you hold back is up to you, but I would recommend saving at least 20% of it, if at all possible, just to be safe.

Rule 3: If you drop all of your classes, you must give back all the money

Let's look at Maria's case again. If she received the full $6,195 and accepts it, and then drops **all** of her classes and does not re-enroll, Maria will be required to pay back the money for those classes if she does not make them up before the end of the academic year.

Remember, when you accept a financial aid grant, you're entering into a contract. To receive the benefits, you must uphold your end of that contract!

Rule 4: You must enroll in at least six hours of classes each semester

Each college or university has some room to set their own financial aid rules, so check with your financial aid office to ensure you understand theirs. However, know that most colleges and universities require students to enroll in *at least six hours* of classes in the longer semesters (fall and spring). These six hours could be combined in several ways, such as:

Option 1:
Two three-hour classes (such as English 301 and Psychology 301)

Or

Option 2:
One five-hour class (such as Spanish 501) and one one-hour class (such as Kinesiology 101)

As long as your total hours for the semester add up to six, you are probably considered in compliance, but, again, double check with your financial aid to ensure!

Financial aid offices may also require that you only take classes that count toward your major or area of study. So, for example, if you are majoring in accounting and your degree plan has no physical education classes on it, if you enroll in two three-hour P.E. classes, your financial aid office may deny you the money. At that point, you could pay for the physical education classes yourself, or drop those classes and enroll in classes approved by your degree plan.

Rule 5: You must make Satisfactory Academic Progress (S.A.P.)

Let's first go over what S.A.P. is, according to the U.S. Dept. of Education[2]:

Satisfactory Academic Progress

You have to make good enough grades, and complete enough classes (credits, hours, etc.), to keep moving toward successfully completing your degree or certificate in a time period that's acceptable to your school.

Each school has a satisfactory academic progress policy for financial aid purposes. To see your school's definition, check your school's website or inquire at the financial aid office. It will tell you:

- What **grade-point average** (G.P.A.) you need to maintain
- **How many classes** you must take each year or semester
- **How many credits** you must complete by the end of each year
- **How often** your school will evaluate your progress
- **What happens if you fail** to make SAP
- Whether you are allowed to **appeal** your school's decision
- How to **regain eligibility** if you lose it

Rule 6: You must re-apply each year for financial aid

Most financial aid offices require students to re-apply for financial aid every year. Happily, though, you won't have to start all over and do the entire FASFA again. This **Renewal F.A.F.S.A.** application is a much quicker, easier version of the F.A.F.S.A. because your information rolls over from last year. You'll just need to update any new information (such as change of address, etc.), and add the current year's tax information.

For more information on the Renewal FASFA and how to submit, visit your financial aid office and/or visit: https://fafsa.ed.gov

Let's now go over our next form of financial aid: scholarships.

SCHOLARSHIPS

Scholarships are very popular, since they almost never have to be repaid. They can and do come from many sources, including:

- Employers
- Schools
- States
- Cities
- Private businesses and other organizations

Scholarships are usually awarded on merit or financial need, but they are also often based on student characteristics (such as age, gender, race, religion, nationality, political affiliation, or even medical history).

They are also often based on future career choice, athletic ability, religious affiliation, or even ancestral heritage.

However, before you rush to apply to scholarships, let's go over a few cautions about scholarship scams, which are becoming increasingly prevalent.

Below, you'll find some danger signs that might indicate scholarship scams[3], according to *U.S. News & World Report*.

POTENTIAL SIGNS OF SCHOLARSHIP SCAMS

- **Application fees:** Even if it's just a few dollars, legitimate scholarships do **not** charge fees
- **No phone number:** Scholarship scams will **not** give out phone numbers because they're too easy to trace
- **No proof of past winners:** Most legitimate scholarship providers love to share stories about past winners and their successes, so no history of past winners is suspicious
- **Requests for personal financial information:** *Never, ever* give a scholarship committee your credit card, bank account, or social security number. If you get a phone call from someone claiming that they need this information to process an application, disconnect the call immediately—and report it
- **Winning a scholarship that you didn't apply to:** If you get a call or email announcing you've just won a scholarship, but you never submitted an application to that scholarship, it's probably a scam

---

Happily, though, there is some good news regarding scholarships: Most likely, you have connections to some business, organization, government, school, or other entity that awards scholarships!

You might have to dig to find them, but often it's well worth it to do just that. In the appendix of this book, you'll find a list of scholarships offered exclusively to adult students, but check other places as well, including the potential sources listed below:

Your elementary, middle, and high schools
- Many have alumni scholarships

Your parents', grandparents', or kids' schools
- Many schools offer scholarships exclusively for their students' or alumni's parents, grandparents, and/or children

Your college or university itself
- Many have prospective and current student scholarship funds

Your department at your college or university
- Many departments have insider scholarships for their students, so if you are majoring in psychology, for example, check with the psychology department

Your employer
- Check to see if your employer offers tuition reimbursement, tuition assistance, or other financial aid programs. If they don't, see who is in charge of this policy and request they begin such a program to reward hard-working employees like yourself

Your church and/or religious/spiritual affiliations
- Even if your church or spiritual group does not offer scholarships, dig deeper. There are scholarship funds that award money exclusively to Catholics, Non-denominational Protestants, Buddhists, Pagans/Wiccans, Native Americans, etc.

Your bank, credit union, or other financial institution
- Many banks and credit unions offer scholarship opportunities exclusively to their members

Your personal groups
- AARP, NAACP, Boy Scouts, Girl Scouts, Toast Master's, American Legion, and many other groups, offer scholarships exclusively to their members
- If you are not a member of any groups, consider joining some!

The Web
- Of course, the Internet offers you ample opportunity, too, but it can be overwhelming to comb through them all, so you'll find a suggested list at the end of the chapter

Let's now turn to our final type of student aid: Loans.

STUDENT LOANS

You may have heard horror stories about student loans, stories of students getting into hundreds of thousands of dollars in debt and perhaps of students having their paychecks garnished to pay back these loans. Sadly, some of these stories are true, but the good news is that even if you do indeed need to get a student loan, there are many ways you can reduce the amount you owe. And, the chances that you'll need hundreds of thousands of dollars in loans are low.

As you've probably guessed, **a student loan** is a monetary award that you must pay back—*with interest*. For this reason, grants and scholarships are obviously preferable to taking out a student loan. However, many of us do need to take out loans to offset the cost of our educations, so if you need a loan, just be wise about how you handle that loan.

For example:

- **Only borrow as much as you need**
    - If you're offered $10,000 but really only need $5,000, then only take the $5,000
    - Sandy Baum, an economist who studies financial aid for the College Board, has these recommendations:
        - Keep your debt low enough that you spend no more than 10% of your post-graduation income on the student loan bill[4]
            - In other words, if you expect to make $80,000 per year after graduation, then don't take out more than $8,000 per year in student loans.
            - If you're not sure how much you'll earn, go to this site: collegescorecard.ed.gov.
    - Baum also recommends you align student debt with your expected income upon graduation. In other words, a theatre major should take out less debt than an engineering or computer science major.
- **Spend the money as if it's yours—because it is**
    - Don't view the loan as "free" money; it's not. Remember, you'll be paying it back—with interest
- **Economize—and only spend on school-related expenses**
    - Books, tuition, supplies, a computer, gas, food, and similar items are needed for college, so using student loan money to fund these purchases is fine
    - Movies, concert tickets, expensive new shoes, vacations, and other luxuries? No
- **Save as much as possible before enrolling in college**
    - Every dollar you save is one dollar less you'll have to borrow
- **Don't enroll at overpriced, expensive universities**
    - State colleges are often just as high quality, if not higher, than the pricier, private institutions, so compare tuition prices

- Use a tuition payment plan
  - The sooner you pay off that loan, the less interest you'll repay
- Be sure you are <u>a resident</u> of your college's state and county
  - Non-residents pay double, sometimes even triple, the tuition residents pay, so if you plan to move, make sure you're not moving out of district
    - Some community colleges have odd districting lines, so a move even just across the street could mean you're now "out of district." Double, even triple, check what's considered "in district" before you move

Student Loan Scams

Just as there are companies who try to scam students with promises of fake scholarships, there are also companies peddling fake student loans and/or loan services, too. They may try to get you to take out a loan, or try to convince you they can help you get rid of your current loans.

How to Identify a Student Loan Scam[5]

Below, you will find some red flags identified by the Department of Education (ED) to help you identify a loan scam.

- **They require you to pay up-front or monthly fees for help**
  - It is illegal to charge an up-front fee for this type of service
    - If a company requires a fee before they actually do anything, that's a huge red flag—especially if they try to get your credit card number or bank account information
- **They ask you to pay *them* directly, instead of your student loan servicer**
  - This is almost always a scam, as they'll simply pocket the money and pretend to pay your loan—they'll do this until you notice, and then they'll disappear with your money
- **They promise immediate and total loan forgiveness or cancellation**
  - Government forgiveness programs require many years of qualifying payments and/or employment in certain fields before your loans can be forgiven
- **They claim they can get you a "special deal" on your loan repayment**
  - Student loan debt relief companies do not have the ability to negotiate with your federal loan servicer for a "special deal" under the federal student loan programs. Payment levels are set by federal law
- **They ask for your FSA ID**
  - **Do <u>not</u> give your FSA ID password to anyone. Ever. Don't allow anyone to create an FSA ID for you, either**
- **They ask you to sign and submit a power of attorney**
  - **Never agree to this. Report this company immediately**

- **Their communications contain spelling and grammatical errors**
  - While many of the communications sent out by these companies look very formal (for example, fold-and-tear letters with safety patterns), they often contain spelling and grammatical errors
  - If you notice unusual capitalization, improper grammar, or incomplete sentences in the communication you receive, it's a red flag

How to Apply for Financial Aid

Now that you understand the various kinds of aid and the scams associated with them, let's cover how to actually apply for aid.

You essentially have two choices:

1. Apply with help

   Or

2. Apply on your own.

Many students prefer getting help from a professional, but it's certainly not required. Choose whichever method works better for you.

1) **Apply with help: Go to your college's financial aid office and make an appointment**
   When you arrive, be sure to bring with you:
   - Your S.S.N. (Social Security Number)
   - The most recent year's tax return
   - If you're under 23 and unmarried with no children, have your parents' tax return(s) ready as well
   - If you're married, have your spouse's tax return handy as well

There are also many community organizations that offer F.A.F.S.A. help, but just be sure they are reputable. Protect your social security number and financial student aid ID (FSA ID) like you would your bank card and pin.

> **Never tell *anyone* your FSA ID, and never let anyone create your FSA ID for you!**

Even if the person is helping you fill out your FASFA, they still should not know your ID and pin. (If they know this information, they can log in as you and take out loans in your name!)

2) **Apply on your own:**
- File the most recent year's taxes and have that information ready
- Get on a secure computer—you're going to be entering your social security number and birth date
- Go to https://fafsa.gov/
- Click on the button "Start a new F.A.F.S.A."
- Follow the instructions given

Deadlines

Each state has its own deadlines for applying for financial aid, and some schools have their own as well, so check with your school, state, and/or financial aid adviser to be sure you apply well before the deadline. The earlier you submit your application, the closer you are to the front of the line—and the quicker you'll be approved for aid. If you wait, it's still possible you'll get your funding, but it's also possible all the funds will be gone, and you'll have to wait until next year.

If that happens, don't despair. Simply apply for that next year immediately so you're first in line for the next school year.

Using Your Money Wisely

As you well know, college is expensive, so saving money when and where you can will really add up over time. So, let's go over some ways you can do just that.

Since books are so expensive, let's begin with ways you can save on books in particular.

Although you likely have a campus bookstore where you can purchase your books, note that the campus bookstore is the *most expensive* place to buy books.

Happily, there are many other places to check besides the campus bookstore, which we'll go over on the following page, but if you *must* go to the campus bookstore, look into these options:

- **Shop around for the best price**
  - Not all campus bookstores have identical prices; often, there is a Co-Op bookstore that offers better prices, so check around.
- **Get a used book when possible**
  - Used books are often half the price of the new ones
- **Look into a paperback edition**
  - Don't assume you need the most expensive, hardback edition. If paperback is available, it's probably much more affordable.
- **Check into digital versions and renting**
  - E-book versions are almost always more affordable, so if you don't care about having the physical book in your hands, see if an e-version is available

- Rentals are often the lowest-cost version of the book; just be sure to return it on time by the end of the semester!

For more affordable alternatives for textbooks, see the chart on the following page.

SAVE MONEY ON COLLEGE TEXTBOOKS

- **Textbook assistance and scholarship programs**
  - Many colleges and even businesses offer funds to help students pay for textbooks, so inquire—at your school *and* at work!
- **Buy an older edition**
  - The newer the edition, the more expensive it is, so check for older editions; they'll cost a fraction of the brand-new book
  - Check with the professor to ensure an older edition is okay (it's probably not ok in science, technology, or medical classes, but in most classes, it's usually fine!)
- **Check libraries**
  - Check your college's library and your local public library; sometimes, you can check out textbooks for the *entire* semester!
- **Check discount websites**
  - Ebay.com
  - Craigslist.com
  - Textbooks.com
  - Amazon.com
  - Betterworldbooks.com
  - Chegg.com
  (Be sure to allow for delivery time!)
- **Check discount bookstores and thrift stores**
  - Discount bookstores and thrift stores offer textbooks at a fraction of the cost of your campus bookstore. Try stores like **Half Price Books, Goodwill, and Savers**
  - You may have to dig at the thrift stores, but often it's worth the time
- **Ask around**
  - Many students post notices regarding textbooks to buy, sell, or trade. These notices might be in-person (on student boards or in the lunchroom, etc.) **or** online via hubs where students are buying, trading, or selling textbooks with each other
  - Talk to other students in the class; see if they have the book you need, or if they might know someone who does

---

In addition to saving money on textbooks, there are ways to save money on tuition, fees, and general living expenses, too.

A Few More Money-Saving Tips

- Be sure you are **a resident**
  - Your tuition costs could be cut in half, so be sure to check the residency status of any place you consider living
- Take **"basics" at your local community college**
  - Tuition is often a quarter of university cost
- Go to **free events**
  - Instead of going to expensive movies or other shows, check your campus or community for free entertainment
- Check into **student discounts**
  - Movie theatres, bookstores, restaurants, and other businesses often give student discounts, but often you must ask for the discount (and present your student ID)

Beware Degree or Diploma Mills

Degree or diploma mills are organizations that award non-accredited degrees or diplomas, meaning their classes are not officially recognized by the proper **accreditation** agencies.

To be properly **"accredited,"** a college or university meets the standards of the Council on Higher Education Accreditation (also known as "CHEA") or the U.S. Department of Education.

Any school can *claim* it is accredited (and degree mills almost always do!). However, the school must be accredited by the *authorized*, proper accrediting agencies. If the school is not accredited properly, your degree will not likely have any value on the job market, and your classes probably won't transfer to other colleges and universities. (For more information on transferring, see Appendix D.)

Be sure to check that your school is accredited properly. Here's how:

CHECK YOUR SCHOOL'S ACCREDITATION:

- **U.S. Department of Education database:**
  - https://ope.ed.gov/dapip/#/home
- **Council on Higher Education Accreditation:**
  - 202-955-6126 or http://www.chea.org/
- **Consumer Fraud Reporting:** http://www.consumerfraudreporting. org/Education_Degree_Scams_Recognize.php

---

Before we close, let's cover one final topic on financial aid: How to get the best return on your investment.

Return on Investment (ROI)

A college degree is an investment—an investment of time, money, effort, and energy. Because you're going to invest so much in this degree you seek to earn, it's important that you understand how to get the most return on that investment, or the most bang for your buck so to speak.

This return is known as ROI, or return on investment (ROI). Essentially, there are two ROIs to consider: financial ROI and emotional ROI.

Let's start with the **financial ROI**.

There are three factors to consider when evaluating the financial ROI of your degree.

1) **Cost of degree**
   What's the total cost of the degree? Be sure you add up *everything*:
   - Tuition
   - Books
   - Fees
   - Gas (to and from campus)
   - Supplies (calculators, binders, pens, pencils, etc.)
2) **Debt you'll acquire**
   How much total loan money did you (or will you) take out?
   Sometimes, students only spend $5,000 on direct school expenses, but then they take out a loan for, say, $10,000 to help cover living expenses (rent, electricity, medical bills, etc.), so be honest here.
   Subtract any grants or scholarships you received.
   You only need to know **how much you'll have to pay back**—and **don't forget to include the interest.**
   If you're not sure how to calculate this, get online and search for a "student loan calculator" to help you, or visit your financial aid adviser for help.
3) **Future earnings**
   Do your homework and research how much you're likely to earn with your new degree.
   Here are some suggested tools to help you figure this out:
   - **College Measures:** Helps identify fields of study and careers with a high return on investment
     - Visit https://air.org/project/college-measures
   - **College Score Card:** See the earnings of graduates broken down by school and program.
     - Visit https://collegescorecard.ed.gov/

- **The Hamilton Project**: Shows average earnings over an adult's working life by type of degree
    - Visit https://hamiltonproject.org/charts/career_earnings_by_college_major/

It's also important to factor in the *emotional* return you'll receive for all your hard work in college. This return is your **emotional ROI**.

To calculate your emotional return on investment, find answers to these questions:

1) **What type of work will make you happy, or at least not make you miserable?**

    Doing a job you hate for eight hours a day, five days per week for years on end is *not* good for you, nor is it good for anyone else. Your friends, family, co-workers, and community will all benefit from you being happy and fulfilled—even if it means making a little bit less money. Don't waste your life energy working somewhere you hate just so you can bring home a bigger paycheck.

2) **What type of work are you good at doing?**

    Being *good* at your job is critical, too. The feeling of completing a good day's work is such a great one that it can get you through some very hard times. In the long run, if you're doing work you really aren't great at doing, you won't advance, anyway, and you'll probably be unhappy. This isn't to say you shouldn't try something new and seek to become skilled in something you're not currently great at doing. You should! But, if after receiving training and experience you're still not improving, it might be time to reconsider.

3) **What inspires and excites you?**

    Doing work that inspires you and aligns with your core values as a human being is an incredibly rewarding experience. If you honestly couldn't care less about teaching others, then please don't go into teaching simply because it offers a good retirement package! Instead, look for work that ignites your passion and gets you excited.

    Granted, it can be difficult to find a career that offers you a high financial ROI *and* emotional ROI, but finding this balance is worth the effort. You'll be working in your field 40 hours per week, every week, possibly for *decades*. So, it's worth the time and effort to make sure your degree is going to pay off for you in the future—both financially and emotionally. You'll be glad you did, and so will your friends, family, and community!

Suggested Exercise

1) Explain the differences between scholarships, loans, and grants
2) If you haven't already, make yourself a budget for the semester, even for the entire year. Include all items needed (rent/mortgage, gas, insurance, phone, electricity, tuition, books, clothing, food, credit card bills, etc.). Get a definitive number of how much money you need to pay for everyday living costs *and* your education.
3) Brainstorm some ways that you could potentially save some money. For example, could you eat at home more? Commute to work with a friend? Cut down to one or two streaming services (instead of five or six)?
4) If you haven't already, apply for financial aid. Visit your financial aid office or go to https://studentaid.gov/h/apply-for-aid/fafsa and see if you qualify
5) Skip ahead to the index on adult student scholarships (Appendix B). Make a list of at least five that you will apply for, and get started applying. Break the process down into manageable steps. For example, first, put the deadlines on your calendar. Then, write out the steps you'll need to take to complete each application (such as write the essay, getting recommendation letters, etc.). Then, decide which steps you'll take and in what order. Enlist the help of a family member, friend, or professor to help you stay on track.

Notes

1 See the basic eligibility criteria here: https://studentaid.ed.gov/sa/eligibility/basic-criteria
2 https://studentaid.gov/understand-aid/eligibility/staying-eligible#satisfactory-academic-progress
3 Read the full article by Emily Kerr here: https://www.usnews.com/education/best-colleges/paying-for-college/articles/2019-04-01/how-to-avoid-scholarship-scams
4 Read the whole article here: https://www.usnews.com/education/best-colleges/paying-for-college/articles/2009/06/09/how-much-money-should-i-borrow-for-college
5 Source: https://studentaid.ed.gov/sa/repay-loans/avoiding-loan-scams#identify-scam

5 What Your Professors Expect You Already Know—But You Probably Don't

IN THIS CHAPTER, YOU WILL LEARN:

- What professors expect of you—and what you can expect of them
- Questions you should—and should *not* ask—your professors
- How to avoid coming across as a lazy, unprofessional student
- What to do when you miss class
- How to avoid being accused of plagiarism (cheating)

Few students want to anger or frustrate their professors. After all, the professor is the one holding the grade book, and everyone knows it. Yet, as an instructor in higher education for more than 15 years, I can tell you that many students have irritated my colleagues and me over the years. Usually, the students didn't mean to do that, but whether they meant to do it or not, sadly, they did.

Some of the offenses students commit are minor, while others are more serious. Yet, even the minor ones can impact your relationship with the professor, which can affect your learning, and ultimately your grade.

Conversely, meeting—even exceeding—your professors' expectations can positively impact your learning and your G.P.A., so let's go over what your professors expect to make sure you impress, rather than anger or annoy, them.

PROFESSORS' EXPECTATION #1:

Students Will Read the Syllabus Carefully to Understand all Course Policies

Some professors will go over your syllabus (which outlines the course description and rules) with you on the first day of class, but others will not.

Whether your professors go over the syllabus with you or not, the information within it is crucial—and they will expect you will read the syllabus thoroughly and ask if you have questions.

To most professors, silence from students equals understanding.

Yet, sadly, so many students glance at the long syllabus their professor gives them, toss it into a folder, and never look at it again.

This is a mistake. Big. Huge.

Why?

The course syllabus is the rules of the game so to speak. If you don't know the class's rules, then how can you "win" (i.e., earn an "A")?

The syllabus will outline crucial information, such as:

- Expected in-class behavior (such as participation level and type expected)
- Grading standards
- Penalties imposed for missing classes and/or arriving late
- The professor's office hours and location
- Textbooks, supplies, or course packets needed
- Assignments and due dates (and the weight of these assignments in your final grade)

After reading over your syllabus, be sure you can answer the following questions:

- **Will you write any papers in this class?**
  - If so, when are they due?
  - What percentage of your grade will each paper comprise?
  - Does the professor drop your lowest paper grade?
- **Will you take any tests in this class?**
  - If so, when?
  - What percentage of your grade will each test comprise?
  - Does the professor drop your lowest test grade?
- **Will there be quizzes?**
  - If so, are they announced beforehand, or are they surprise ("pop") quizzes?
  - What percentage of your grade will each quiz comprise?
- **Will you take final or mid-term exams?**
  - If so, when?
  - What percentage of your grade will each exam comprise?
  - Are these exams cumulative?
- **Is attendance/participation required in class?**
  - If so, how many classes must you attend?
  - What are the penalties for missing class?
  - If "active participation" is required in class, how is that defined?

- **Will homework be graded?**
    - If so, what percentage of your grade will each homework assignment comprise?
    - Is the homework graded on actual accuracy of responses, or is it simply graded on whether or not you attempted all items?

PROFESSORS' EXPECTATION #2:

Students Know it Is *Their* Responsibility to Ask Questions When They Don't Understand

---

In high school or GED classes, most instructors probably went out of their way to make sure you understood all the material. They probably asked you an endless list of questions and gave you worksheet after worksheet to test that understanding. In college, that's not likely to be the case.

Professors will lecture over the material, often racing through it at lightning speed. They expect that you, the student, will ask questions about anything you do not understand. Remember, to most professors, silence means understanding.

If you're nervous about asking questions, that's understandable. Perhaps you wonder if your question is "stupid" or not, and you don't want to irritate the professor. It's good of you to consider the professor's feelings, but consider your own as well. You are a student in the class, and you have every right to ask questions. In fact, you have a responsibility to do so—not only to yourself but to the other students in the class, too, and even to the professor herself. One of the best ways we (professors) can judge whether students understand is by their questions. If I give a lecture on, say, thesis statements, and I get 12 questions from students, then I know I did not cover that material very well, and I need to return to it.

Besides, if you have a question about something you're learning in class, it's likely the other students have the same question. They just aren't brave enough to ask it!

I know it's hard to do, but if you have questions, summon up your courage, and ask them. This is tricky for many students, so let's go over how to formulate your questions so you'll feel more comfortable asking them.

How to Formulate Questions in a College Class

- **Make sure it's an actual question**
    - NO: "I don't understand."
    - YES: "Would you please repeat that definition?"

- Aim for specificity—don't be vague
  - NO: "Huh?"
  - YES: "Would you please explain where the number 245 came from?"
  - YES: "Why must I place my thesis statement as the last sentence in the introduction paragraph?"
- Ask only one question at a time
  - Don't pepper the professor with lots of questions *during* class. He'll probably find that frustrating, and so will other students
  - If you have many questions, write them down and save them for after class or office hours
- Time your questions well
  - Don't interrupt the professor to ask a question
    - Wait until there is a natural pause, and then raise your hand
  - Most good professors will say, "Any questions?" That's your moment! Speak up!

If you're not comfortable asking questions in front of the whole class, see the professor before or after class, or visit office hours. If you have a teaching assistant, consider approaching him/her as well. If there's an "A" student in your class that you feel comfortable approaching, ask him/her your questions, too. Rather than being annoyed, they'll probably be flattered you noticed their aptitude in class! The tutoring or learning lab at your college or university is yet another potential source of answers for your questions.

Lastly, remember that **talking to you—the student—is an important part of the professor's job.** Students often worry that showing up to office hours or sending emails with questions is "bothering" the professor. It's not! In fact, communicating with students is, for most of us, the best part of our jobs! It's the reason we went into teaching—to be able to communicate with and help students. We teach for a reason, and you (the student) are the biggest part of that reason, so don't hesitate to seek help!

PROFESSORS' EXPECTATION #3:

College Students Are *Professional* Students

One of the biggest expectations professors have of college students is that they understand college is the "big leagues" so to speak. In other words, professors expect you will behave as a pro, which (to them) means you:

- **Take the class seriously**
  - Arrive on time
  - Listen when the instructor talks
  - Take notes
  - Do the required work and turn it in on time
  - Don't expect special favors or think the professor "owes" you anything
  - Look interested in the class material
    - Make eye contact while the instructor teaches
    - Nod and smile when appropriate
- **Respect the class**
  - Arrive on time and stay for the entire class
  - Be courteous to your fellow students and instructor
  - Never speak while the instructor speaks
  - Don't text or be on your phone/computer/tablet during class (unless you're taking notes)
- **Actively engage in the class**
  - Complete all work assigned—whether it's being graded or not
  - Ask questions
  - Offer answers/opinions when the instructor asks for it, but don't dominate discussions. (Give other students a chance to speak, too!)
  - Bring notes and books to class with you and look over them while you're waiting for class to start (Yes, we notice when students do this!)
- **Have a good attitude**
  - If the instructor asks you to do group work, do it
  - Don't roll your eyes or behave as though you're really put out by something the instructor says or asks the class to do
- **Know what's going on in class,** *whether you were absent when the work was assigned/due or not*
  - If an assignment is due, and you tell the instructor you were not in class, the response you will get is likely this: "So?"
  - It is **your** responsibility—as the student—to know what work is assigned in class and when it's due, whether you were present the day it was assigned or not
- **Reach out when you're absent to discover if any new assignments were given or due dates changed**
  - Contact the professor, your TA, and/or other students to ensure you didn't miss any new deadlines or testing dates if you're absent from class
  - Check your online platform (Google Classroom, Blackboard, etc.) to see if any announcements were posted

- Be an overall professional
  - Turn in your work on time
  - Check your student email account regularly and respond to email in a timely manner (preferably within 24 hours)
  - If your professors use an online platform (like Blackboard or TRACS), check regularly (at least weekly) for any announcements
  - Follow the dictates of all assignments: Do *exactly* what the instructions direct, no matter how demanding (or annoying!) they are
  - Don't turn in sloppy, lazy work; do your best
  - Don't cheat

PROFESSORS' EXPECTATION #4:

Students Will Not Ask for Information Already Given to Them on the Syllabus or Other Course Documents

---

You may initially be confused here because, after all, we discussed earlier the importance of asking questions. Yet, the distinction here lies in *what questions you are asking*. Emailing to seek further help on an assignment or to ask clarification questions is good—great, even. However, to email a professor to ask for information you could easily find yourself is not fine.

Let's go over some examples to be sure you understand the difference between questions you should, and should not, ask.

Question	Should you ask?	Why?
When is Paper 2 due?	NO	This information has already been given to students (on the course calendar and probably the assignment itself). To ask for it makes it seem you are too lazy to check your class documents. (Unless, of course, the instructor made a mistake and didn't include it. In that case, be sure to mention that you checked the course calendar and assignment sheet, yet you can't find the due date.)
Do I have to take the final exam to pass the class?	NO	All grading information should be listed on the syllabus, so check there before asking. If it's not there, then you may ask.
When are your office hours?	NO	Again, this information is almost certainly listed on the syllabus. (If it's not, then you may ask.)

(Continued)

(*Continued*)

Question	Should you ask?	Why?
I'm having trouble understanding how to apply the formulas in Chapter 5. Would you be able to help me during your office hours this week?	YES	This is a question regarding class content and understanding, so definitely ask this one!

Here's the bottom line: If you have a question, double check all your course documents and class notes to ensure the professor did not already provide this information.

PROFESSORS' EXPECTATION #5:

Students Understand They Need to Study about three to six Hours Outside of Class, on Top of Class Time

Unlike your job, school is not over when class is. In fact, the work has really only just begun when you leave class! This is a hard fact for many new students to learn, especially adult students. We're used to leaving our work behind when we "clock out," but as a college student, most of your learning will happen *outside* of class.

If you aren't reviewing your class notes, reading your textbook, and working on class material outside of class, then you're likely not doing well in the class. Showing up for class lectures is great, but it's not enough in and of itself. There's simply too much information to learn in the space of class-time, so it's imperative you work outside of class to learn it.

The information is also high-level, which means you'll almost certainly need to review it several times to deeply understand it.

Hearing it once in class won't be enough, so be sure you're taking notes and reviewing them often.

PROFESSORS' EXPECTATION #6:

Students Understand That We Are Their *Instructors*, Not Their Friends

As an adult student, many of your professors might be your age, or perhaps even younger than you are.

Some students mistakenly think this similarity in age means they can call the instructor by his/her first name.

This is not the case.

The instructor's age has no bearing on the title ascribed to her, and as the instructor, **she** will determine how you address her. If she expressly invites you to call her "Mary," then you may certainly do so. Otherwise, it's Professor Smith, or Dr. Smith, accordingly.

Many adult students also often mistake professional courtesy with friendliness. You can expect your instructors to show general interest in you, meaning asking you questions about yourself and your goals, sharing funny jokes or stories with you, and generally showing concern about your wellbeing. However, what you should *not* expect is that the two of you will become friends. Exchanging personal phone numbers or extending invitations to "hang out" in settings outside of the college environment are not appropriate.

Once the semester is over and you are no longer enrolled in his/her class, it would be fine to pursue a professional friendship, particularly if you are hoping to enter the professor's field. However, always err on the side of formality here, and keep interactions professionally friendly. Remember, always call him/her "Professor" or "Dr." and his/her last name, *not* "John" or "Mary"—unless expressly told you may.

PROFESSORS' EXPECTATION #7:

Students Will Use Professional Correspondence Via Email

Because both you and your instructors are so busy, it's almost certain you will need to communicate via email during the semester. When this occasion arises, take your time to compose a professional, clear email. You would probably be amazed to learn how many wildly inappropriate and/or utterly unclear, confusing emails students have sent over the years. These kinds of emails harm you as a student because when you send them, one of two problems will occur:

1) The instructor will be so irritated by the unclear or unprofessional email that he/she will simply not respond to it.

   OR

2) The instructor will have to send an email asking clarifying questions, which means you will then have to write *another* email to explain your original email!

In both cases, you lose because you've wasted your precious time—and the professor's. You also unfortunately make yourself appear to be a sloppy, unprofessional student.

Here's how to avoid this scenario:

1) **Give your email a specific, pertinent subject title that includes your course number**
   - Don't type the entire message in the title line—only the title goes in the title line
   - Use keywords to help you title the message so its content is immediately clear to readers

---

YES EXAMPLES:

1) Message Title: "Eng 1301 (Section 22343): Student Mary Martin Absent Today"
2) Message Title: "Hist 1431 (Section 34648): Student John Preston Requesting Meeting"

Both of these "yes" titles include the student's name, course number, and the reason for the email. Professors are likely to respond to these emails.

NO EXAMPLES

1) Message Title: "A Question"
2) Message Title: "Help!"
3) Message Title: "I need help with understanding the lecture better in class, so can you please help me to do better in some way?! I'm really willing to work hard; I just need some extra help. Thank you!"

The first two message titles are entirely too vague and give the instructor absolutely no idea of the email's subject matter. The last one is too long—the student has typed the *message* where only the *title* should be.

2) **Use a greeting and direct address**
   - Extend an appropriate, professional greeting
   - Use the professor's last name and title—unless he/she expressly gave you permission to use his/her first name
   - Don't just start typing the message—greet the reader first

YES EXAMPLES
"Good Morning, Professor Gill—"
"Hi, Professor Gill—"

NO EXAMPLES
"Hey,"
"Charlene,"
"I'm really having trouble in class and wanted to see if you could help me."

The "yes" examples all offer an appropriate, professional greeting. The first two "no" greetings are too informal, and the last message offers no greeting whatsoever. It just jumps right into the message, which most professors will probably consider rude.

3) **Identify yourself immediately**
   - Most instructors have hundreds of students, so don't assume your instructors know who you are!
   - State your full name and the class in which you are enrolled

YES
"My name is Mary Cervantes, and I am a student in your T/Th English 1301 class at 2:00 p.m. at Riverside Campus."

NO
"This is Darcy. Can I come to your office?"

In the "yes" example, the student is perfectly clear about who she is (a current student) and which class she is in (the T/TH 2:00 class at Riverside). Now, the professor has context for the email, which makes it more likely she will answer it. The "no" example is vague and unclear. The professor will wonder, "Who is Darcy? Is she a current or former student, or is she even a student at all?!" Not exactly a good start.

4) **Email *only* from your official college email address**
   - **Never** send a professor an email from an inappropriate email address (such as hotloverforyou@yahoo, etc.)
   - Memorize your official school email address and password, and log in regularly
   - Email *only* from this account for all matters pertaining to your schoolwork!

5) **State your question or concern clearly—and be as specific as possible**
   - A professor will only respond to your email if you are clear and direct.
   - If you offer a general statement, such as, "This material is really hard for me," you've given the professor no room to answer a question.
   - It's fine to say that you're struggling, but then follow up with a question or a specific concern the professor can address

NO	YES
"I can't really understand what you're teaching." "This class is really hard for me." "Can you help me?" "I'm lost."	"Would you be willing to take a look at my draft of Paper 2 during office hours tomorrow? I'd like to see if I'm going in the right direction." "Would you be able to meet with me during your office hours on Thursday to go over our quiz from today's class?"

The "no" examples give the professor no question to answer, but the "yes" examples do, and they also suggest a specific time to address the problem.

6) **Use proper punctuation, grammar, and spelling in your email**
   - Mistakes are forgivable and understandable, but sloppiness is not!
   - Check and double check that email before sending it, *especially* if you're writing your English instructor!
   - Write in complete sentences, and use a formal tone.

If you need a refresher of proper English writing rules, invest in a good writing manual. (I recommend *Essential Writing Skills for College and Beyond*, Penguin ISBN 10: 1599637596, ISBN-13: 978-1599637594.)

PROFESSORS' EXPECTATION #8:

Students Will Never, Ever Ask This Insulting Question: "Did I Miss Anything Important When I Was Absent?"

If you recall the questions we discussed earlier that you should not ask, please add this one to the top of the list: "Did I miss anything important when I was absent?"

Here's what the professor wants to say in response: "Oh, no, you didn't miss *anything* important. Since you were not here, we just sat around and discussed what type of smoothies we all like best!"

Of course you missed a great deal of important information when you were not in class! To ask whether you missed "anything important" implies that there are times when information is presented that is *not* important. See the problem here?

The very question is insulting to the professor—and the class overall.

Instead, what I believe you meant to ask is something such as:

- "Professor, I missed class on Tuesday, and I just wanted to verify that all assignment due dates have remained the same?"
- "Professor, I missed class last week because I was sick, and I see on the course calendar that we were scheduled to cover X, Y, and Z and read pages x–y in our textbook. I have read all of these pages and familiarized myself with X, Y, and Z via both the text and a fellow student's notes. Are there any other resources or anything else you recommend I do to ensure I am fully caught up?"

PROFESSORS' EXPECTATION #9:

Students Will Not Ask for a Higher Grade Than They Earned

Some students seem to feel that if they simply show up to class regularly, then this means they should pass. That is not the case. To pass, you'll have to turn in all assignments, attend class, participate, and earn passing grades on all assigned work.

However, if you study hard, go to class, and *still* end up with low grades on assignments, then you may have a valid concern. Write out your case and gather your evidence (papers, quizzes, assignments, etc.). Then, if you feel it's worth the effort to talk to the professor, do so, but tread carefully here.

If you're arguing a "D" paper is really a "B" paper, you'll need a strong, strong case—and you'll want to proceed cautiously.

Few professors will take lightly a student who questions his grading abilities.

Grading is by no means a science, especially in an English, history, or philosophy class, so if you want to develop a long-term relationship with this professor, be careful how you ask about your grades. Instead of demanding to know, for example, why your essay was an 87 (instead of a 97), visit office hours and share with the professor that you want to excel in the class and master the material. Focus on *learning* and *improving*, rather than simply on raising the score. This way, you come across as a student who truly wants to learn and grow, rather than one who only cares (and wants to argue) about grades.

If, after speaking with the professor, you still feel he is being unreasonable or unfair, take your case to his supervisor (usually the department chair). Occasionally, a student really does have a valid problem to point out with a cantankerous professor. However, I can tell you from experience that usually when there is a grade dispute, it is because the student feels grades should be *given* and not earned. So, be sure you're not feeling that way before you go to the time and effort of disputing the grade.

The other reason for grade disputes is if you encounter an error. Professors make mistakes, too, so if you know your final course grade adds up to a 91, and your grade is listed as a "C," then you need to reach out to the professor. (Just be sure to have all your graded work ready to show to the professor!)

For this reason, *always* check your official posted final grades every semester. Never just assume they were entered correctly—and **always** keep all work from your class until you see that official, correct grade posted at the end of the semester.

PROFESSORS' EXPECTATION #10:

Students Understand that 9:00 Means 9:00

In the American higher education system, if your class is listed as beginning at 9:00 a.m., then that is exactly what time the class begins—not 9:04 or 9:09.

In fact, the professor may likely walk into class at 9:00 on the dot, already lecturing.

That means at 8:57, you should already be in your seat, with notebook and pen/pencil out, ready to begin. Don't saunter in with your coffee at 9:07, thinking that class begins around 9:00ish. Nine a.m. means 9:00 a.m.

This is important not just for the professor but also for you. If you're late, you'll probably miss important information. (Many professors, including myself, make important announcements at the beginning of class on purpose to reward on-time students.)

Besides, it's actually quite rude to show up late to the class. No matter how quiet you are, everyone notices when someone walks in late, and it disrupts the flow of class. So, please be courteous to your fellow students and arrive on time. Your instructor and classmates will appreciate it!

PROFESSORS' EXPECTATION #11:

Students Understand They Must Cite All Their Sources in Their Papers

---

Many beginning college students think it's perfectly fine to take information they found on a website, cut and paste it into their own document, and then turn that paper in as their own—without acknowledging that they took this information from another source. Let me assure you that this is **NOT** fine! In fact, it is cheating.

This form of cheating, or **plagiarism**, is actually theft of intellectual material, and it is a serious offense. Depending on how severe the theft is, it could cause the student to fail the assignment or the entire class. Some colleges and universities may expel students with repeat offenses, so double check to be sure you cited all your sources.

If you're not sure how to do that, see the MLA, APA, or Chicago Style handbooks for more information, or ask your instructor, teaching assistant, or tutoring lab to help you. If you make mistakes citing, you may lose a few points, but if you don't cite at all, you'll likely fail the assignment. For this reason, it's better to cite incorrectly than not to cite at all!

PROFESSORS' EXPECTATION #12:

Students Will Notify Their Professors of any External Factors That Might Be Affecting Their Performance in Class

---

Often, students think professors are cold, heartless people who could care less what is going on in their lives. Happily, this is not the case!

Most professors care deeply about their students, so if one is going through something traumatic (such as a divorce, custody hearing, job loss, increased shift load at work, etc.), then they want to know about it.

Even if the problem is not necessarily academic in nature, if it's affecting your ability to do well in class, then your professor should at least be aware of it.

Granted, you don't need to launch into a 30-minute diatribe in which you outline the 4,000 ways in which your ex-spouse is trying to steal from you in the divorce settlement! However, you can let the professor know you're going through a difficult time personally, and it's leading to trouble with studying and/or concentrating. You can give further details or not—that's up to you. Often, once the professor knows there are extenuating circumstances, she will likely check up on you or offer to give you an extension on assignments.

Just be sure you don't take advantage here.

If the professor gives you an extra week, don't ask for three. Then, be sure that you actually complete the assignment and turn it in by the new deadline. And please don't go announcing your new deadline to other students, either—be discrete—and, of course, thank her profusely for helping you!

If you're ever uncertain of a professor's expectations of you, visit office hours and politely inquire. Most professors only wish their students would take such an active interest in their education!

Suggested Exercise

1) Gather your syllabi from all your classes. Re-read them, and then use each to sketch out answers to the questions outlined at the beginning of this chapter. If you're not enrolled in college classes yet, do a Google search for "college syllabus" and your favorite subject (English, math, etc.). Choose 2–3 of the syllabi you find and use them to answer the questions listed above.

2) Rewrite the email below so it is clear, specific, and professional. (Be sure you give the professor questions to address.)

From: CStudent@communitycollege.edu

To: Professor Smith@communitycollege.edu

Subject: Freaking out!

I'm so scared about the test on Friday. I don't know what to do. I'm going through a crazy divorce, and I am hoping you might help me a little bit during office hours to get caught up with the other students?

Thx!

---

3) Make a list of questions you have for each of your classes. Then, search your syllabus and other course documents (calendar and handouts, etc.) for answers. If you can't find answers, email your professors and request a meeting during office hours to go over all your questions. If you can't meet during the professor's office hours, email him/her and suggest an alternative time. If you're not yet enrolled in a college class, make a list of the questions you might ask the professors of the courses whose syllabi you found.

Section II

Achieving Your Academic Dreams—Step by Step

6 Select Your Classes and Professors Wisely

IN THIS CHAPTER, YOU WILL LEARN:

- What degree requirements are and how to meet them
- The differences between "credit" and "developmental" classes
- What classes you should take, at what time, in what order—and why
- Tips to move you to the *front* of the registration line
- How to find the best professors

Many new students simply enroll in whatever classes are available or the ones listed first on their degree plan. Other students let their adviser decide their classes, blindly enrolling in whatever the adviser recommends. Both of these strategies often lead to big problems later.

Your adviser no doubt means well, but he can't possibly know you better than you know yourself. This is why it's critical that you take the time to study your degree plan and requirements for yourself to ensure *you* understand them. Then, you can plan the perfect schedule for *you*.

Granted, some classes are **prerequisites**, meaning that you *must* take them before taking later courses, but for those aspects of your schedule that you can control, control them! Your personality, schedule, and learning abilities are like no one else's, so your course pairings should reflect and complement that uniqueness. Listening to sage advice is important, but it's equally important to listen to yourself.

Let's go over, then, what degree or certificate requirements are, and then we'll cover how to use them to create your perfect schedule.

Degree or **certificate requirements** are those requirements spelled out by your college or university that *must* be met for you to earn your degree or certificate.

Let's begin with degrees, and then we'll cover certificate requirements.

Degree Requirements

Most colleges and universities require you meet three major criteria to earn a degree: You must earn a certain number of credit hours, be in residency for a certain number of hours, and maintain a minimum G.P.A. (See below for further details).

1) **Credit hours**
   - Every degree will have **a minimum number of credit hours** you'll have to earn before the school awards you a degree.
     - For an **Associate's degree**, you must earn approximately 60 credits (20 classes at three hours each)
     - For a **Bachelor's degree**, you must earn approximately 120 credits (40 classes at three hours each)
   - Every degree will also have the minimum credit hours organized within categories, and you must earn credits within each category. Typically, there are three categories: General Education, Major-Specific, and Elective Credits:
     - **General Education Credits** (also called "Gen Ed" or "Core Curriculum" courses)
       - Also often called "basics"; these include classes such as English, history, math, science, government, etc.
       - These classes will comprise anywhere from one third to one half of your entire coursework, depending on your college and/or major
     - **Major-Specific Credits**
       - These are the courses in your specific major. For example, if you major in criminal justice, these classes would probably include criminal psychology, corrections, criminal investigations, etc.
     - **Elective Credits**
       - These are courses you can select yourself, but often with parameters
       - Double check with your department to ensure any elective you take is approved to count toward your degree! (Art history probably will, but underwater basket weaving? Probably not!)
2) **Residency Requirements**
   - Most colleges or universities require that you complete a certain number of credits with them (at *their* college or university), before they award you a degree.

- For example, if I took 115 hours of credits at Boston College and then transferred to Harvard and took only five credits there, Harvard would *not* issue me a degree. Even though I met their 120 hours total credits, I did not take enough credits with *them* (Harvard).
- Each college has its own rules for how many hours you must take "in residency," so if you plan to transfer, be sure to see how many credits you need at the new school to earn the degree. (See Appendix D for more information on transferring to a university.)

3) **Minimum G.P.A.**

- Usually, a G.P.A. of 2.0 or higher is needed to graduate, but each school or department has its own rules, so verify with your school/department.

Certificate Requirements

For certificates, the requirements are typically much more lenient. Usually, coursework focuses entirely on the selected major. No Gen Ed or electives are usually required, but check your certificate plan and/or with your adviser to verify.

For example, a certificate in welding would require *only* welding courses—no English, history, or government classes are likely required.

Now that you understand your degree/certificate requirements, you'll need to know whether you must take any developmental classes (also known as "zero level" classes).

Developmental (or "Zero Level") Courses

Developmental classes are refresher courses that build your foundation within a certain subject (such as reading, writing, or math). These classes are also known as "zero-level" classes because you will not earn any college credit for completing them. They're just below the college level because they are designed to build students' skills and knowledge to help them reach the college or "credit" level.

Whether your college requires you to take these classes is likely determined by your college or university's "**placement exam.**"

A placement exam assesses your current knowledge level in reading, writing, and math. If you do not earn a certain score on this exam, your college may require you to take developmental classes before you can take credit-level classes.

If you are indeed required to take these courses, don't panic!

Millions of students all over the country need these classes, especially students who have been out of school for many years. Needing refresher courses is **not** an indication of intelligence or ability to succeed in college. It simply means you may need a bit more foundation building before you start the more rigorous college classes.

If that's the case, it's better to invest time in building a firm, solid foundation than to rush into credit courses you're not quite ready to take.

If you're interested in learning more about these types of classes and the primary differences between them and "regular" college classes, see the chart below.

Developmental vs. Credit-Level Classes

"Zero-Level" or "Developmental" Classes	*Credit-Level Classes*
• **No** college credit is earned because the material taught is not quite at the college level • You can use your financial aid to pay for these classes, but *be careful*! Don't use up all your financial aid on these classes! • Even though you don't receive college credit, your grades in these classes often still count toward your G.P.A., so take them seriously!	• College credits are earned toward your degree or certificate • You can almost always use your financial aid or scholarship awards to pay for these classes, as long as they are listed on your degree or certificate plan. (If you're not sure, check with an adviser.) • Your grades in these classes will always count toward your G.P.A. • Your grades are crucial for financial aid purposes, and certainly if you plan to transfer to a university or earn a post-graduate degree

Alternatives to Developmental Classes

Many colleges and universities offer alternative programs that can be quicker than the traditional developmental track. Depending on how many developmental classes you need, you may want to inquire about these "fast track" options, such as College Prep or Intensive Programs.

If your college *insists* on you taking the developmental classes, yet you really believe you're ready for credit classes, simply re-take the assessment test. Once you earn the required score, you can then take credit-level classes.

You can also speak with a dean or your department chair. Sometimes, they grant students permission to bypass these classes. This, of course, is rarely granted, but I have seen it happen, so it doesn't hurt to ask.

Enrolling in Your Classes

Once you complete those developmental classes, you're ready to enroll in credit classes that count toward your degree. Just be careful here. Many students blindly enroll in any college math class they want, thinking it doesn't matter which particular one they take.

This is *not* the case!

Each degree plan has its own specificities regarding *which specific* math or science or history classes you must take.

For example, are you to take English Composition, college algebra, and biology?

Or,

Are you to take American literature, statistics, and physics?

Check that degree plan and/or ask your adviser to ensure you are enrolled in *precisely* the correct courses that count toward your degree.

Once you understand what your degree requirements are and what courses you need, let's start choosing those classes and professors! We'll begin with the classes and then move on to the professors.

Choosing Classes

---

1. **Examine all available options carefully**

    Most colleges and universities offer hundreds, possibly thousands, of courses each semester. You can see what those options are by looking at your school's course schedule.

    To find your college or university's course schedule, go to the school's home page and type in "course schedule." If you can't find it, ask for help via the chat line or your adviser.

    Once you find the course schedule, look over it and make a list of the classes that interest you.

Some students make an old-school list in a notebook, while other students go high-tech and create a spreadsheet by copying the information from the course schedule itself and then pasting it into a blank spreadsheet document.

2. **Plan, plan, plan!**

Don't wait until the day of registration to see what classes are open and then try to piece together a schedule. Be proactive; plan out your potential schedule(s) in advance. Classes fill quickly, so prepare a plan A—your favorite schedule—as well as plans B, C, D, and even E.

This way, you're ready to roll out your best plans the second registration opens.

Most colleges open registration based on seniority, so if you're a new(er) student, you'll probably register *last*. However, the good news is that you can invest this extra time in planning!

When considering your plan for classes, consider the following points:

- **How many classes?**

   Most adult students are in a hurry and want to take as many classes as they can, as quickly as they can. Yet, this is often not the best plan in the long run. Granted, it takes longer to graduate if you only take one or two classes per semester, but it's slow and steady that wins the day, not racing with panic to the "finish line."

   In fact, I've found the students who burn out are almost always the ones trying to blast their way through college. They load up on four or five courses per semester, and these classes, along with their 40-hour work week, plus home life, proves to be too much. So, they burn out. On the other hand, students who take their time and enroll only in a class or two each semester graduate successfully. It takes longer to get there, yes, but they do get there, and they earn honors while doing so. Even more importantly, they *enjoy* their college classes and learn a great deal, all while still maintaining relationships with loved ones.

   I know you're in a hurry, but please consider taking your time rather than rushing.

   If you're thinking that you *can't* take your time because in three years you'll be 67 or 48 or whatever age, let me assure you of something: You'll be that age, anyway. Wouldn't you rather be that age and have a college credential under your belt, one that you actually enjoyed earning?

- **Pair the right classes together**

   Some subjects work well together, and others don't. So, think carefully before you sign yourself up for anatomy and physiology, English Composition, and calculus in the same semester. These are three decidedly difficult, high-maintenance courses. It can be done, of course, but it'll probably mean a *very* stressful semester!

> Expert students have learned a better way:
>
> They pair a hard class with an easier one.

Experienced students know that the extra hours needed for the hard class will not be a problem because they won't need to invest as much time in the "easy" class.

> Remember, though: "Hard" and "easy" are relative terms!
> To one student, a history class might be very easy and a math class hard.
> Yet, to another student, the math class is easy and the history class is hard.
> So, just be honest with yourself. Which classes might require a great deal of your time, and which classes might require less time?
> If you're not sure, err on the side of caution here.
> Remember that you have to factor in not only class time but study/homework time, too.

(If you're a second-language learner, beware classes with heavy reading loads, such as psychology, history, sociology, and English.)

- **What day(s) of the week?**

  Most college classes will be offered on either two or three days of the week. For example, many students choose classes that meet on Mondays and Wednesdays (MW) or Tuesdays and Thursdays (TTh). If you can, try to schedule all your classes on the same days so that you're not commuting to and from school four or five days per week. That 15, 20, or 30-minute commute *each way* adds up quickly, so pack the classes together, if possible.

- **What time(s) of day?**

  Ask yourself: At what time of day are you at your peak for learning? Early morning? Late afternoon? Evening?

  Then, be realistic about what you can accomplish and when.

  If you're best in the early morning, but you have two kids you must shuttle to two different schools by 8:30 a.m., then it's probably not feasible to sign up for a 9:00 a.m. class. Even if you can make it to class by 9:00, you'll likely be stressed out from your drive and not in the best frame of mind for learning. A 9:15 or later class would probably be preferable because then you'll have a cushion for completing or printing any assignments and/or reviewing notes. Plus, you'll be more relaxed and better prepared to learn by the time class starts.

Remember, too, that your "peak" time might depend on the subject. Perhaps you're great in the morning for your job, but you absolutely detest doing math before noon. Scheduling an algebra class at 7:00 a.m. three days per week, then, might not be the best idea.

- **Breaks between classes?**

  Beware long breaks between classes in which you might be tempted to waste time. A 30-minute break might be ideal so you can study or review notes, but two hours? If you have classes two days per week, that's *four hours* per week! If you would truly use those four hours to study, great, but if they'll be wasted, try to reschedule.

- **Be realistic**

  Only **you** know if you'll actually show up to that Biology class at 7:15 a.m. every Monday, Wednesday, and Friday. Maybe you will, but maybe you won't. No one knows but you, so **be realistic** when you're scheduling classes.

  Don't sign up for a class just because it looks good on paper. Ask yourself if you are really, truly going to go to that class each time it meets and be ready to learn, with homework completed and notes reviewed by the start of class.

  For example, if you work 8:00 a.m.–5:00 p.m. and must take night classes, your adviser may want to sign you up for two back-to-back classes from 6:00–10:00 p.m. On paper, that seems like a good schedule, but ask yourself if that schedule will actually work logistically. Can you really commute from work to school in just one hour and have all your work completed and ready to turn in? What about dinner? What about picking up the kids? Can you really be in class until 10:00 p.m.? When will you complete homework? When will you spend time with the kids?

  Perhaps you have solutions to these questions, and if you do, that's great, but if not, you'll want to plan out logistically how the schedule will work in the real world—*each* week for an entire semester.

  Consider, too, the location of the class.

  If two classes you want are available but located far apart, can you actually make it to both classes? Many community colleges have locations all over town, and a class offered at one campus could be miles away. On university campuses, you'll often have to walk from one class to another, so be sure you check to make sure you can physically make it from one class to the next in time. Factor in traffic, parking, climbing stairs, broken elevators, etc.

- **Online or in-person classes?**

  Many students like the idea of taking a class exclusively online. After all, they can work at their own pace, and there's no need to fight traffic, rush to get a parking spot, or hurry to make it to class on time. However, these classes can be tricky to navigate because you don't get the in-person interaction with your fellow students and instructors, and often instructors in these classes are not as responsive as students would like. (Sometimes, it can take up to 48 hours to get a response to a question.)

If you decide to take an online class, **be sure you do your research on the professor** *first.*

Unfortunately, some instructors teach online classes because they think they're "easier" than the in-person class. The result? Students receive less attention and help. Of course, not all instructors feel this way, and many do excellent work teaching classes online. Just be sure you enroll with a professor who teaches well online so you learn everything you should.

- **Move to the front of the registration line**

  Check with your adviser to see if you qualify for early registration. If you're in a highly specialized major or affiliated with a particular department, often you are allowed to register early—but only if you're aware of this privilege.

  Also, some schools allow returning adult students or first-generation students to register early, too, so check to see if your school offers such a program. If they don't, suggest it!

  Additionally, if you make friends with an adviser, sometimes they might just register you early him/herself. Granted, not all advisers at all schools have the power to register you early, but some do, so politely inquire.

  If you are registering yourself, when registration day comes, be sitting at your computer, ready to log in and register the *second* registration opens. Don't delay! The most popular classes can fill in just minutes.

Choosing Your Professors

Many students enroll in a class based solely on the subject matter, the time it's offered, or the location. Yet, there is another critical factor to consider when deciding on which classes you should take: the professor.

The right professor can make all the difference for you—either positively or negatively.

A hated subject can become tolerable, even likable, with the right professor at the class's helm. Similarly, a beloved subject can become detestable with a cranky or simply incompetent professor.

I wish I could tell you that colleges and universities carefully screen all professors to make sure they are encouraging, inspiring individuals who are the best, most effective teachers in their field—and that they absolutely love students and love teaching.

Sadly, this is not the case.

It should be, and hopefully in the future it will be, but right now, it's not, so beware.

There are a few bad professors out there, many so-so ones, a few good ones, and even fewer great ones.

Obviously, you want the great ones! The question is: How do you find them?

1) **Read professors' reviews**

   Look up professors on **ratemyprofessor.com** and read their reviews. Pay attention to key words or phrases that are important to you. Don't just read a review or two, but read them all. Get an *overall* sense of the students' opinions of the professor and his/her fairness, teaching ability, and course policies. If there are a few disgruntled students, that's fine, but are *most* students happy with the quality of instruction?

2) **Sit in on classes**

   The best way to get a sense of which professors work best for you is to try out their classes. If it's a big class at a larger university, you might be able to just slip in and listen. If it's a smaller class or at a community college, you'll probably have to email the professor and request permission. (Or, if the professor teaches with the door open, you could always sit in the hall and eavesdrop!)

3) **Be on the lookout for the great ones**

   Many colleges and universities now have large, public teaching centers or enormous computer labs where there are many classes going on simultaneously. If you see professors who look engaging or interesting to you, grab a seat nearby and listen in. Find out what she teaches and then see if you need that class and could enroll in a future semester.

4) **Look for online video course samples**

   Many professors offer free videos of their lectures on YouTube, both for their students and for general users. See if any of the professors you're interested in taking offer these videos, and watch.

5) **Ask your fellow students**

   See if other students have taken a course you're planning to take. If so, they are a great resource for helping you find great professors. Just be sure to ask follow up questions to see *why* the student liked the professor. After all, what one student likes, another may not, so keep in mind that *one* rave review isn't quite enough information. However, an overwhelming chorus of positive comments might be.

6) **Ask your current favorite instructors and/or adviser**

   Most of the great professors know each other, or at least know *of* each other, so if you like one or two of your current instructors, ask them for recommendations. Advisers, too, are good sources for professor recommendations, as they often get word-of-mouth reviews on professors straight from their students.

Suggested Exercise

1) Explain the differences between developmental and credit courses.
2) Write about the worst class experience you've ever had. Be as descriptive as possible. Why was it so bad? Then, brainstorm ideas for how you can ensure you avoid repeating the experience.
3) Write about the best class experience you've ever had. Be as descriptive as possible. Why was it so great? Then, brainstorm ideas for how you might repeat the experience.
4) Review the questions for planning your perfect schedule. Then, answer them for yourself. What time of day are you at your peak? What days work best for you for classes? And so on.
5) Get on ratemyprofessor.com and look up some potential professors whose classes you might take. Or, get with a few fellow students, an instructor, or your adviser and ask for recommendations for professors.
6) Use your answers to the questions above to create your perfect class schedule for next semester.

7 Master Work/Life/ School Balance

IN THIS CHAPTER, YOU WILL LEARN TO:

- Eliminate time wasters from your schedule
- Get organized
- Win family, friends, and employers' support for study and class time
- Carefully craft your ideal schedule so it *actually works* for you

---

Finding the balance between being a student, working, and spending time with friends/family and/or with your hobbies is often the most challenging part of being a student.

So, how can you succeed in college and still do your job, raise your kids, *and* enjoy your life?

The answer is this: Learn to achieve *balance*.

The bad news here is you probably won't ever figure out how to achieve *perfect* balance. Yet, the good news is that you can achieve *greater* balance in your life. Let's go over the steps to doing just that.

Remember Your "Why"

Working toward a college degree takes *years*, so it's easy to get discouraged along the way. It can get frustrating to watch your coworkers get to go home at 5:00 p.m., but you must rush to school to study and work hard until 9:00 or 10:00 p.m. several nights per week, plus study on the weekends.

At these times, remind yourself **why** you're going to school.

Why are you here, working so hard?

Why is college important to you?

What is it you hope to achieve?

You could be going home and watching TV or hanging out with friends/family, too, but you *chose* to go college. **Why?**

When you remember your goals and dreams and the *reasons* behind them, it will help you keep going when you get frustrated. Write these goals down, and remind yourself of them often—daily, even hourly, if need be!

Keep these goals and dreams close to your mind and heart—and to your eyes and ears, too. Put inspiring pictures, music, or quotes on your phone, in your books, on your desk, or wherever you need them. This way, when you need some inspiration, it'll be there.

Set Your Priorities

What it is, exactly, that you want to achieve, not only in going to college, but in life overall?

You want to get a college education, yes, but you probably also want to achiever a higher *quality* of life, do you not? Isn't that the real, deeper reason behind getting a college education—to live a better life?

> If so, ask yourself what that quality life looks like.
> It probably contains much more than just a better job.

Does it also include a healthy mind and body? Might it also include strong, positive relationships with others?

If so, then you need to nourish all of those areas *now* so that you'll have them upon graduation and beyond. That graduation event will be so much more rewarding if you achieve this balance than if you blow through college at top speed only to realize you reached the finish line alone and stressed out.

Think carefully, then, about your priorities—school, work, friends/family, etc.

List them all out. Then, rank them in order of importance, starting with number one and working your way down.

Remember, this list is for *you*, not anyone else, so don't worry if other people will judge what's on your list or the way you've ranked it.

It's *your* list, not theirs, so just be honest.

And, don't worry right now about how to fit everything into the schedule. We'll get to that. Right now, just focus on identifying your true priorities.

Eliminate Time Wasters

Another key to achieving balance is to identify time wasters. We all have them. The question is: What are yours?

Everyone's time wasters are unique to them, but let's go over some of the most common time wasters to give you some ideas of what yours might be.

Many students immediately cite watching TV, surfing the Internet, or checking social media as time wasters. Although these things *might* be time wasters, they can also be very enjoyable and relaxing.

The key to knowing if things or people in your life are time wasters is this:

DETERMINE WHAT VALUE THE ACTIVITIES ADD TO YOUR LIFE.

The benefit you receive should be greater than or at least equal to the amount of time you invest in them.

For example, you might be tempted to call TV watching a time waster. Not so fast.

Do you deeply enjoy watching TV? Does it make you laugh, relieve your stress, and give you a respite from work and stress?

If so, then TV watching might actually be adding great value to your life. However, if you're watching four or five hours per day, then perhaps you can *reduce* how much you watch.

This point equally applies to social media and the Internet (YouTube videos, Instagram, etc.).

If you're investing three hours per day in TV watching, Internet surfing, and social media, can you cut it down by an hour? Instead of investing three hours, how about just two? If you did, you just found seven hours per week.

Cutting just *one* hour per day from media watching frees up **seven extra hours per week!**

Just this one simple act of reduction could be enough time for you to take an entire college class.

Remember: You're In Charge

Your life is *yours*, so don't let other people dictate how you should or shouldn't spend your time. If other people believe you should constantly be on social media so you can "like" every post or picture they share, that's not a fair ask.

Similarly, if they expect you to attend day-long events every month when you have tests and papers due, you'll need to negotiate. You may not necessarily need to stop doing these activities entirely, but you will need to *reduce* how much time you spend doing them. Instead of attending for seven or eight hours, how about just two or three? You could then invest the other five or six hours in studying and relaxing.

Take some time and make a list of your potential time wasters. To help you get started, here is a list students often make when we do this activity in class. These activities may or may not be time wasters for you. Only you can determine that. Just be honest with yourself and determine what activities (and perhaps people) in your life are time wasters.

Possible Time Wasters

• Excessive TV & movie watching and/or channel surfing	• Playing video games or watching YouTube videos	• Excessive social media use
• Going to movies/happy hour/clubs, etc.	• Spending time w/ negative friends/family/coworkers	• Gossiping/complaining with coworkers
• Emailing, texting, and/or constantly checking phone	• Extended Internet surfing	• Excessive shopping
• Attending useless, unproductive meetings	• Keeping up with celebrity culture and "news"	• Sleeping in/oversleeping

Cutting time wasters can be difficult, especially if the time wasters are people. So, do it gradually, and do it with kindness. There's no need to be disrespectful to anyone, but at the same time, remember that if you keep a time waster in your life, you're dishonoring yourself—and all the people you could help in the future.

Find Pockets of Time

The more mindful you are of time wasters, the more you'll realize this truth: *Every* minute counts.

If you can't find several hours per week of time wasters, start with finding several *minutes*. You might be surprised to see how quickly just a few minutes per day can really add up over time.

For example, if you find just 20 minutes per day, you just discovered

- 2.3 extra hours per week
- 10 extra hours per month
- 37 extra hours per semester
- 121 hours per year

These are hours you could study, spend time with kids, exercise, or just relax—rather than waste time on activities that aren't moving you closer to the life you want.

Here are a few more examples of places you could potentially cut or reduce time wasters. Remember, just a few minutes here and there can add up quickly.

- **Sleeping in**
  - Instead of sleeping in on weekends, why not give up that luxury and rise an hour and a half earlier to eke out some extra study time?
- **Waiting at the bus stop/dentist office, etc.**
  - Instead of sitting at the bus stop, dentist, or mechanic's garage and doing nothing (or checking Facebook!), bring your schoolwork and use that time to study. Bring flashcards or class notes, or download a study app and use that time wisely.
- **Binge TV-watching**
  - Rather than binge-watching that exciting new series on Hulu for four hours, watch just an episode or two, and then invest the other two hours in finishing up math homework or starting an essay. (The episodes will still be there next week—or even at the end of the semester as a reward for your hard work!)
- **Getting phone alerts**
  - Turn off Facebook, Instagram, email and other notifications that come directly to your phone. You don't need to know every second of the day who is messaging you. Set times to check messages, and unless there's an emergency, stick to those times and those times only. If you're constantly checking your phone, you're distracted, so turn it off!
- **Not pre-prepping meals**
  - Instead of making or buying meals every morning, noon, and night, pre-prep as many of them as you can. This way, you can grab and go in the morning, and you don't have to figure out what's for lunch/dinner later, nor will you have to wait in line at the drive-thru or elsewhere. When you make your own food, you'll probably eat healthier, too, and save money. (For example, many students like making a huge pot of spaghetti, soup, or stew on Sunday and then eating it for the rest of the week. Experiment and see what works best for you.)
- **Not delegating**
  - Instead of trying to do everything yourself, make the kids and other family members help you. If you have teenagers who drive, have *them* run the family's errands, and let the younger kids take out the trash and do other easier activities for you. It's good for them to learn to contribute to the household; plus, it'll save you time and frustration.

Get Organized

Once you learn to say "no" to everything that doesn't belong in your schedule, it'll be much easier to get organized, which is absolutely crucial for achieving balance in your life—and for succeeding in college.

The question, though, is *how* to get organized, so let's go over some top tips:

a) **Keep all school stuff together, in one place**

Have a regular place where your backpack, notes, and books will be. Ensure it's clear to family members that your stuff is *off limits*! Your books and supplies are not toys, so kids are **not** allowed to play with pens, pencils, highlighters, etc. (Get them their own, so they won't be tempted!) If your school items are always in the same place and ready to go, you'll save precious moments—and much frustration—searching the house when it's time to leave or study.

b) **Charge phone and computer each night**

The last thing you need is to arrive at school, ready to study or take notes, and your laptop or phone dies on you. Instead, be proactive, and make sure all your devices are charged and ready to go by the time you get up in the morning. And, spring for an extra phone charger and keep it in your bag or car, just in case.

c) **Keep supplies well stocked**

Be sure you've got plenty of paper, pencils, pens, and notebooks. You don't want to have so many that your backpack weighs four tons, but at the same time, you also don't want to waste five minutes digging through your bag for a pen that isn't there.

d) **Get a planner/calendar—and actually use it!**

Most planners will divide up the day, week, month, and even year for you, which will help immensely with making sure you understand what is due and when. Most email accounts come with a free calendar that you can sync with your phone, and you can even turn on notifications that will alert you when important deadlines are near. Old-school paper planners are great, too, so just find a system that works for you, and use it to help you stay organized—and on time!

e) **Budget time for *each* class**

How much time you need for each class is something you'll only know once you begin the class, but, in general, you'll need to budget *six hours per week total per class* (three hours in class, three hours studying outside of class).

This is a just general guide, though. You may need a little more or a little less, depending on your skill level in that subject. (We'll discuss schedule-making in greater depth shortly.)

Keep papers organized

Many students' struggle with organization stems from keeping up with all the paperwork that comes with college (class calendars, syllabi, paper prompts, worksheets, test reviews, and handouts, etc.), so let's go over some ways you can successfully manage all that paper.

Tips for Organizing Paper

(Handouts, study guides, course syllabi, etc.)

Use Quality Binders:

- Get yourself a sturdy, durable binder or folder for **each** class
- **Don't** go cheap here
  - Avoid the cheap, flimsy 15¢ folders that fall apart
- Get dividers and then file the different types of documents within each section:
  - Course syllabus and calendar
  - Homework assignments
  - Paper prompts
  - Study guides
  - Handouts (formula sheets, diagrams, etc.)

If you don't want to keep up with multiple binders, you could potentially keep all papers from all classes in just *one* binder, but make sure you get one that is large enough, and have a clear system for finding papers quickly and easily.

Color Code:

- Get a different color folder/binder/spiral for each class
  - For example, your purple binder and purple spiral notebook could both contain English documents and notes; your red binder and red notebook contain your math notes

Master Electronic Storage:

- Make an e-folder for each class on your computer, in your Cloud, or on your Drive or USB
- Title all documents clearly (such as "English 1301 Paper 1 Final Draft")
- Drag all important documents into the appropriate folder (be sure you place only English class documents inside the English folder and so on)
- Decide if one folder for each class is enough, or if you want to have folders within folders. For example, your English class folder may have sub folders:

- **English Class Folder**
  - English Syllabi and Course Calendar
  - English Homework
  - English Essays
  - English Class Handouts

Another key to achieving greater balance is developing a support system.

Get Key People In Your Life On Board

If absolutely no one in your life (friends, family, employer, etc.) is on board with your new schedule/life plan, the chances of your success are small. True, you can do it alone, but when you have others pulling for you, it's much easier (and enjoyable), so let's discuss how to win the support of others.

Get Family and Friends on Board

Be clear from the start with your partner, extended family, or close friends on several things:

- What you're trying to accomplish and why
- How and when you're going to accomplish it
- What you need/expect from them to help you

First, outline the ways in which education will benefit your entire family. It will help you get a better job that brings in more money, sure, but it's more than that, isn't it? Your education will get you a *career* (rather than just a job), which will help you acquire work you actually *like*, which will help you be happier and more fulfilled.

You'll also be better equipped to help the kids with their homework and to advocate for them at school and in the world at large.

Second, be clear with your family and friends about your school timeline. If you think your education will take two or three years, be honest about that fact. Two years is a *long* time to a small child, but it's important you don't jeopardize the relationship by being dishonest. Stress that you're still there for them and always will be, but you won't likely be able to spend as much time with them as you once did—but this is only *for now*, and only during the semester.

Third, when you're with loved ones, give them your utmost attention. Be fully present. Don't text. Don't study. Don't check social media. Just be present. Listen. Enjoy. Connect. Don't allow any distractions. Make every second count. It's quality over quantity.

Also, do your absolute best to make it to the big events. You can always make up study time, but you can't make up missing someone's sweet sixteen or 50th wedding anniversary.

Lastly, outline the specific ways that you would like family members and friends to help you. For example, perhaps it's obvious to you that no one should call or text you while you're in class, and that the kids should pick up their rooms and clean the kitchen for you. Yet, this may not be obvious to them, so whatever your specific needs or expectations are, outline them in advance to ensure everyone is on the same page.

Aside from avoiding misunderstandings, if you're honest from the start, your friends and family will understand that they are a key part of your plan. In exchange for their help and support, thank them often, and include them specifically when you speak about future plans so they'll understand you're not envisioning a future that excludes them!

Get Your Employer on Board

An employer who understands your goals and how they pertain to the work you do for them will almost certainly help you arrange a flexible work schedule. Even if you don't plan to get a degree in the particular field in which you are currently working, your education will undoubtedly help you become a better thinker and learner, which makes you a more valuable worker because you'll bring these skills to work each day.

If an employer doesn't agree, then you do indeed have a problem. You will want to ask yourself why you're working so hard for an employer that either fears your betterment or is indifferent to it.

Clearly, getting a new job is not an option for everyone. However, if your employer refuses to work with your school schedule, you may want to consider going with a kinder, more supportive employer. College is hard enough; you don't need a grumpy employer to worry about, too.

Another important key to achieving balance is to reduce time with "crabs."

Reduce Time With Crabs

You may have heard this inspiring story: When fishermen trap crabs by putting them into a bucket, the crabs aren't actually trapped. Any of the crabs could easily escape—and some try. However, the other crabs refuse to let the free-thinking crab out of the bucket. They pull him right back down, thus ensuring the entire group's demise (i.e., being cooked by the fisherman!).

The parallel to human behavior—and to your college life—is this: Sometimes, people will attempt to pull you down so to speak, to sabotage your achievements. Granted, they may be acting from a place of genuine concern, worried that you're setting yourself up for a fall. Yet, it's crucial that you kindly tell these people you've made your decision, and you're going to see it through.

If they repeatedly try to stop you or are constantly sharing their "doubts" to try to pull you back into that "bucket," you may need to reduce—or even cut entirely—the time you spend with these doubters. College has enough challenges; don't waste your precious energy with people who believe (or even hope) that you'll fail.

Carefully Craft Your Schedule

The keys to crafting a great schedule are three-fold:

1) **Take your time in creating it**
2) **Be honest and realistic**
3) **Be specific and meticulous**

Don't rush to create a schedule just to get a checkmark that you made a schedule. The whole point of crafting a schedule is to figure out how best to allot your time. You want your schedule to actually work for you, so take your time and do it right.

Be sure, too, that you're honest—and realistic. Don't write a schedule that sounds or looks good only on paper; it needs to actually work in the real, everyday world in which you live. It sounds great to say you'll exercise for 12 hours per week, but can you realistically allot that much time to exercise? It may seem impressive to write on your calendar that you'll rise at four a.m. each day, but **will** you? Only you know for sure, so just be honest.

Specificity is important, too. Be sure you include *all* of your responsibilities when budgeting your time. We often forget how much time we spend on small tasks, such as eating, shopping, parking, fighting traffic, showering, getting dressed, doing laundry, etc.

One of the best ways to identify all of these items is to try The 24-Hour Exercise. (See instructions below).

THE 24-HOUR EXERCISE

1. Choose a typical day in your life, and then write out every single thing you did that day, for the entire 24-hour period
   - Include everything—watching TV, getting ready for work, making lunches, driving to work, standing around talking to coworkers, etc.
2. Get a pencil and scratch out all the stuff that you wasted time on
   - "Wasted" means time spent on things that are not getting you where you want to go in life.

3. Circle or highlight your "keepers"
   - These are the activities you want or need to keep in your life, such as working, spending time with kids/family/friends, commuting, sleeping, getting ready, etc.
4. Declare war on time wasters!
   Make a plan for how you will either **cut** or **reduce** the time wasters in your life—**every single one of them!**

Some students like to do this exercise a few times to make sure their data is accurate, so feel free to try it as many times as you need.

It may also help to think of your time in terms of sizes:

Small = Hourly
Medium = Daily
Large = Weekly
Extra Large = Semesterly
Super Size = Yearly

It's up to you where to start with your schedule (small or super size), but many people find it helpful to start with the biggest items and then work backwards to the smallest.

Yearly Plan

How many credits will you earn this year? What other goals do you have for yourself? List them out—and be as specific as possible. Instead of writing, "I want to take classes," specify *how many* classes you want to take.

If you want to take five classes this year, figure out how you could do that. (Perhaps two classes in both spring and fall, and then one class in the summer?) Or, if you want to save $5,000, *how* specifically could you do that?

Consult that priority list you made earlier to help you list these goals, and then break them down into manageable chunks, perhaps by semester.

Semester Plan

Each semester, enter into your calendar the important dates for each class:

- Class times
- Paper deadlines
- Test dates

Then, confirm with friends/family about any important upcoming events (such as concert tickets or kids' birthday parties, etc.) or other obligations (volunteering at church, taking care of a neighbor's pet, etc.).

If you know your work schedule, enter it as well. If you have any say whatsoever in the days/hours you work, supply your employer with your preferences as soon as possible. The earlier they know your availability, the more likely they'll honor it.

Weekly Plan

To formulate your weekly plan, ask yourself these questions—and be specific:

- You will work from ___to___ (hours) on_____ (days)?
- You will study from ___to___ (hours) on_____ (days)?
- You will spend time with family/friends from ____to____ (hours) on_____(days)?
- You will relax from ___to___ (hours) on_____ (what days)?

Daily Plan

Map out the small-ticket items on your daily schedule and determine the length of time needed for each:

- Working
- Studying
- Class Time
- Commuting
- Picking up/dropping off kids
- Getting ready (showering, dressing, etc.)
- Eating
- Shopping and other errands
- Household chores (cleaning, yard work, etc.)

Hourly Plan

Be realistic here when assigning what you'll do each hour.

Can you *really* get ready in the morning (make lunches, get all papers together, etc.) in only an hour? With traffic and parking, can you *really* get from work to class in 30 minutes?

When making your hourly plan, be sure to consider how much time you can and should devote not only to class but also to studying and completing homework.

Remember the general rule for studying and homework: Spend at least one hour studying *outside* of class for each hour spent *inside* the class.

If you can't find this many hours in your schedule, then you'll either have to cut out some other items, or take fewer classes each semester.

Granted, taking fewer classes will push back your graduation date a bit, but your G.P.A. will thank you—and so will your mind and body because they'll be much less stressed. It's better to take your time and do college right than to rush through it to hurry up and finish.

Adjust When Needed—and Be Kind to Yourself

I wish I could tell you that once you craft your ideal schedule, you'll stick to it every time, but the truth is almost *no one* is able to do that (at least, no one I've met!).

The trick is to stick to it *as best you can.*

Also, be kind to yourself when you're unable to meet your schedule's dictates. Don't panic or beat yourself up. If you missed a deadline because of a mistake on your part, learn from that error and move on. Mistakes happen, so cut yourself some slack and remember that you're still learning. The more you practice, the better you'll get.

Turn Your Schedule into Routine

We humans are creatures of habit, so developing a new routine is *hard*. The first time you have to get up early to study or stay up late to work on a homework assignment will be the hardest because you're changing your routine. Your mind and body will probably rebel!

However, the good news is that this principle works in the reverse, too: Once you establish your new schedule as routine, it'll be easier to stick with it.

The first few weeks—especially the first few days—are the hardest. So, get through those, and the schedule will get easier.

Consistency is the key here, so decide on your best schedule, and then do your best to stick to it.

Within about a month, if you're consistent, this routine will be your new habitual schedule!

Take Care of Yourself

I know this is easier said than done, but please take care of yourself. Don't wear yourself out to the point of breaking so you can "succeed." Sadly, so many students do just that; they wear themselves out physically, emotionally, and otherwise trying to excel in college, and instead, they burn out. The world needs your talent, ingenuity, and contributions, but we won't get them if you burn out.

So, again, please, take care of yourself.

You are important, and you have critical work to contribute to society, so take the time to care for yourself as needed. In the long run, you'll be glad you did, and you'll realize that true success lies not only in taking care of others but also of yourself.

We all have different needs, but in general, do your best to:

- Eat healthy
  - Running to the drive-thru every day is not only expensive but also unhealthy. Try to find alternative foods that are affordable yet quick. (Try yogurt, trail mix, granola bars, cereal, hummus & veggies, peanut butter sandwiches, etc.)
  - Pack your own food when you can, so *you're* in control of proportions
  - Pay attention to what foods your body likes best. If you eat certain foods because they're deemed "healthy," but your body doesn't run well on them, perhaps they're not healthy for *you*
- Don't skimp on sleep
  - Do your best to get seven to eight hours of sleep each night
  - If you can't get the full eight hours, get as many as you can. Sleep helps your brain and body restore themselves, and it also ensures all the information you put into your brain over the day is filed into long-term storage
  - The better you sleep, the better you'll perform
- Find a moment to relax
  - Take a moment or two each day to slow down and enjoy life. Just slowing down for a minute or two and taking a deep breath can really make a big difference to your mental, emotional, and physical health.
  - Set a timer on your phone, and when it goes off, pause and relax. Take a deep breath. Slow down. Don't think. Don't study. Don't work. Just relax. Then, you can get back to work.
- Laugh every day
  - Ever heard the statement, "Laughter is the best medicine"? It's definitely true. So, seek out laughter every day—whether it's with a funny friend, movie, TV show, or cute puppy video on YouTube.
  - Laughing helps you relax, and it relieves stress. So, laugh it up, and do so often!
- Reward yourself
  - College is hard work, so reward yourself often—and not just at the end of the semester!
  - When you study for a few hours or work hard on a project, give yourself a reward. Buy yourself a coffee or iced tea, get a massage, take a bubble bath, drink a glass of wine, watch your favorite TV show, or do some other nice thing for yourself

- Your body and brain will soon learn that they get rewarded for working hard, and they'll be more likely to do it in the future!
- **Celebrate victories big and small**
  - No need to wait until you ace that bio class to celebrate. Did you turn in your work on time? Study hard for that test? Go to every single class this week? Those are all victories, so honor your work by celebrating them. You deserve it!

Suggested Exercise

1. Make your priorities list for this semester and/or next semester. Then, rank them in order of importance.
2. Complete the 24-Hour Exercise.
3. Make a list of your top 10 time wasters.
4. Use the information above to create your perfect schedule.
5. Keep a notebook to log how effective the schedule is (or not!). Adjust where needed.

8 Take Notes Like a Pro

IN THIS CHAPTER, YOU WILL LEARN:

- Principles of successful note-taking
- The top 5 note-taking systems for college
- How to develop your own note-taking style
- How to **use** your notes to become a top student

Many students sit in their college classes and listen carefully to the professor, yet when test time arrives, they bomb the exams. These students are understandably frustrated and ask themselves what went wrong. Usually, they decide they just aren't smart enough to be in college, and often they drop out.

However, the problem is not the student's intelligence. Instead, it was almost certainly this: The student either didn't take notes all, or they didn't take *effective* notes.

You probably already know that one of the most effective ways to remember—and understand—what you're learning in class is to take notes. After all, these notes, if effective, will help you:

- Explain the material to yourself, which teaches you to become a better learner
- Deepen your understanding of class material, and of the professor
- Sharpen your writing, listening, and critical thinking skills
- Reduce your stress for test-taking since you have a transcript of in-class lectures

Most students know all this, but what they don't know is *how* to take notes.

The truth is that taking notes is an art, and it's one learned by practice. Copying someone else's system verbatim probably won't work because the ways in which you explain things to yourself is probably different than the way another learner does.

Yet, there are key principles of note-taking that we'll cover in this chapter that will help you to develop a system that works for you.

Let's go over them, step by step.

Step One: Know What to Write—and What Not to Write

It's impossible to write down *everything* said or done in class, so the first step to successful note-taking is figuring out what to write and what *not* to write. To do that, ask yourself: **What information here is *most* important?**

Each class is unique, so what's important in one might not be in another—your job as the student is to figure out these distinctions in each class. Luckily, there will be many clues you can use to guide you, such as:

- **Studying the professor**
  - The professor almost always tells you, either outright or in subtle ways, what is important. For example:
    - **Pay attention to voice inflections**
    - When the professors stresses certain words by saying them louder or carefully pronouncing them, that's a clue they're important
  - **Notice body language**
    - If the professor gestures grandly or widens his/her eyes when discussing a certain topic, this is a hint that the information is super important. Put a star by this critical info
  - **Write it down, if it's on the board**
    - If the professor takes the time to write it, so should you
    - When the professor underlines things on board, this is a huge hint that it's important
  - **Listening for words or phrases that repeat**
    - If the professor uses the same vocabulary word or mentions a certain formula three of four times during class, you can bet those items will be on the test. Be sure you know that info backwards and forwards!
  - **Paying attention to the professor's overall perspective on the class's material**
    - Example: if you're taking an English class, and the professor goes on and on about the **biographies** of the authors of class texts, then you can bet author background information will be on the test. (*You* may not think the authors' biographies are interesting or important, but if the professor keeps mentioning them, then they'll probably be on the test.)

- Example: If you're taking a history class, and the professor is constantly mentioning one historic date after another, then you guessed it—*dates* will be critical to know on the test! Conversely, if the professor rarely mentions dates but instead often discusses the long-term social impacts of historic events on society, then you should probably focus on those, rather than on memorizing a bunch of dates.

If you're ever in doubt, ask the professor what, specifically, she feels is most important to study for the tests. She may not tell you, but, then again, she might!

Remember, when you're deciding what is important, don't focus necessarily on what *you* think is important, but on what *the professor* thinks is important. (After all, she's the one writing the exam, not you!)

Step Two: Master General Note-Taking Principles

Study the principles below and begin putting them into practice in class immediately.

- **Sit front and center**
  - Aim for that front-row center seat. It removes any other distractions between you and the instructor.
- **Turn off your phone**
  - Seriously. Turn it off. **Do not** use your phone in class
  - Your professors *will* notice when you're on your phone, and if you later have questions, they may not be willing to help
  - It's distracting to you, anyway, so unless you have an emergency, keep the phone *off* and out of sight
- **Read the textbook assignment *before* coming to class**
  - When you come to class having already read the material, it'll make note-taking much, much easier because you'll already have begun the process of understanding it
- **Be brief**
  - *Summarize*; don't try to write down *everything*. You can't! Focus on **key** ideas.
  - Don't worry about grammar, spelling, or punctuation. Granted, your notes need to make sense, but don't waste time putting every comma or period in the right place.

- Focus on *understanding*, not regurgitation
  - Get the overall main ideas; don't worry about writing down the professor's exact words
  - Focus on the major ideas, facts, concepts, and principles
- **Write quickly but legibly**
  - Don't write so quickly that you can't read your notes, but also don't write so slowly that you fall behind
  - Be as neat as you can
    - Skip spaces and use plenty of paper
  - Use abbreviations; develop a standard set that you use in each class
    - Use "ex." instead of "for example"
    - Don't write, "This is important!!!" Instead, just **star** (***), **bold**, or underline it
    - Shorten long names
      - (e.g., Shakespeare becomes Shake; Napoleon become Napol)
  - Take pictures of the board, if allowed
    - If your professor writes a lot of notes on the board, request permission to take a picture of it before she erases it

---

Step Three: Study the Major Notetaking Methods

Now that you have a general idea of strong note-taking principles, let's go over some top methods that have proven helpful to millions of your fellow college students. Try them and see which one works best for you. Feel free to incorporate your favorite elements of each and leave out any that don't work for you. Here's the five we'll cover:

- **The Cornell Method**
- **The Mapping Method**
- **The Outlining Method**
- **The Charting Method**
- **The Sentence Method**

The Cornell Method

The Cornell Method helps you organize material into a clear structure.

How to Do It

1) Divide your paper into three columns—cues, notes, and summary—as shown below.

CUES	NOTES
SUMMARY	

2) Use each section as its title indicates:
   - Use the **cues/clues section** to write down cues/prompts during class that will help for reviewing notes later
   - Use the **notes section** to take notes during class. The bulk of your notes go here
   - Use the **summary section** *after class* to write a summary of the notes from above (Focus only on main points)

Example 1: The Cornell Method

Cues and Clues	*Notes*
Write key vocab and terms in this section.	In this space, record your notes from class. Use **bold**, underline, **s, or ALL CAPS to emphasize key info.
You can also write key **recall questions** in this section, too.	Focus on the **big ideas.** Use an **organizational pattern** that is easy to read and follow. For example, you might want to use bullets and listing.
	• Bullet lists help you keep your white space on the page
	• Bullet lists also make things easier to read
	• You can use subpoints as well
	• These subpoints help you be clear on the relationship between ideas
New Sections	When the instructor starts a new section or topic, skip lines to visually organize the information and keep different ideas separate.

SUMMARY

In The Cornell Method, focus on the **main ideas and organize** the information so it's easy to review later.

- Use bullet lists, **bold**, underline, and/or ALL CAPS for emphasis
- Be brief!

Example 2: The Cornell Method (Mindset Lecture in College Success Class)

Cues and Clues	Notes
Growth mindset	Belief that you can grow your brain and **become smarter.** Trying new, **challenging** things is key; they help you learn and grow.
Fixed mindset	Belief that you can't ever become smarter, *no matter what you do.* You're stuck.
Sayings	Growth: "I don't know how to do this yet, but I can learn." Fixed: "I don't how to do this, so what's the point in trying?"
What are some axioms of each mindset?	• "You've either got it, or you don't"=Fixed • "Practice makes perfect"=Growth • "I'm not a math person"=Fixed • "I'm not a math pro yet, but I'm learning" = Growth

SUMMARY

It really comes down to your goals:

- Growth mindset people's goal is to *become* smarter, so they'll take risks and don't care if other people label them "dumb"
- Fixed mindset won't take risks because their main goal is to *look* smart, instead of *become* smarter

The Outlining Method

As its name suggests, in the **outlining method**, you'll structure your notes in the form of an outline. Use bullet points to represent different topics, with points and subtopics.

How to Do It

1) Write the main topics on the far left-hand side of your paper.
2) Indent and add each subtopic with a bullet point below the main topic.
3) To begin a new main topic, skip a space and return to the far left-hand side of your paper.

Example 1: The Outlining Method

Page number
Today's date

I. Start with the most general idea or **main topic**—the **key idea**—in the lecture
   a   Write **explaining information** for the main topic or key idea here.
      i.   This is a subpoint. It illustrates or gives an example of the explanation given above about the main idea.
      ii. This is another subpoint. You can use it to explain even more, or give another example.
   b   This is **more explaining information**; it still relates to the main topic but deserves its own new thread.
II. When you have **a completely new main idea**, start a new line and add white space between it and the main idea above it, so it's clear you're starting a new idea.
   a   You don't necessarily have to have subpoints or examples on every single main idea. Just write what you feel is most important to remember. (You can always add them later, too, when you're reviewing your notes!)
III. You'll probably have a few of these **completely new main ideas** in each class lecture.
   a   Give yourself some examples to illustrate each main idea when possible to help you remember them.

Example 2: The Outlining Method (English Class Example)

Page number
Today's date

I. **The Thesis Statement**
   a. **Summarizes your essay's position/argument in one sentence**
      i. Be sure it's **arguable**—it should not be a fact
         1. **NO**: There's a debate in our country about whether college should be free or not. (This is a fact, not an argument!)
         2. **YES**: College should be free (This is a *position*—someone could argue with me!)
   b. **Lists your supporting reasons, which you'll examine in the essay**
      i. Ask yourself, "Why?" about your position
      ii. Ex: College should be free because____, ____, and ____.
         1. It would open up more opportunities for more people, pump more money into our economy, and ensure equality for all

    c. **Is the last sentence in the Introductory paragraph**
        i. This way, you have time to set up the essay's topic, then tell the reader your position on it
    d. **Should use specific, defined language**
        i. Avoid vague terms such as "lots of reasons" or "many ideas"
       ii. Don't say vague things such as, "In this essay, I will tell you"
    e. **Must be a statement**
        i. **Don't ask a question—state your position!**
           1. No: "Should college be free?"
           2. Yes: "College should be free."
    f. **Outlines your entire essay**
        i. Readers should be able to tell what each body paragraph will discuss
           1. **Body Paragraph 1:** How free college would open up more opportunities
           2. **Body Paragraph 2:** How free college would pump more $$ into economy
           3. **Body Paragraph 3:** How free college would ensure equality for all

The Charting Method

In **The Charting Method**, you'll use charts and columns to organize information. This method is helpful for lectures that cover a lot of facts or relationships between topics.

How to Do It

1) Divide your page into columns (Use class information to help you determine how many columns)
2) Label the columns with the key main ideas or topics

    For example, in a history class, perhaps your course calendar indicates you'll cover facts on four major wars that day in class: WWI, WWII, Vietnam War, and the Global War on Terrorism. These four wars' titles could be column headings.

3) Fill in the rows with the information from the lecture in the appropriate column.

Example 1: The Charting Method

Today's date Class/main topic			Page number
How does this method work?	*Pros*	*Cons*	*Best times/classes to use it?*
First, make a chart, and then set up your columns and rows	It's a nice way to visually represent information, esp. for comparisons	Some professors are hard to follow, so you may waste time trying to figure out where info goes	Use any class outlines or course calendars of topics to pre-create the categories
Then, insert information (words, phrases, main ideas, etc.) into the appropriate categories	Easier to read than long-winded paragraphs	Doesn't always work for every class or topic, so some students find it difficult to use	*Visually* organizing the info often makes it easier to understand
You may not know the categories in advance, so it may be better to fill them in after class	Helps you see the *relationship* between ideas	Drawing charts in class may be distracting and cause you to miss key info	Many students find this method best for taking notes on textbook readings, not for taking in-class notes

Example 2: The Charting Method (History Class Example[1])

WAR *	*Years*	*Total U.S. Servicemen Deployed*	*U.S. Deaths (in Battle and Other Deaths in Service)*	*U.S. Wounded*	*Estimated Cost to U.S. Taxpayers in $$$ (Adjusted for inflation)*
WWI	1914–1918	4,734,991	116,516	204,002	$334,000,000,000
WWII	1941–1945	16,112,566	405,399	670,846	$4,104,000,000,000
Vietnam	1964–1975	8,744,000	90,220	153,303	$738,000,000,000
The Global War on Terror (GWOT)	2001– present	2,774,000	7,032	52,802	$1,147,000,000,000

The Sentence Method

In **The Sentence Method,** you simply write down *one* sentence to explain each key idea or topic discussed in class. This method works well for fast-paced lessons in which the professor covers a lot of information.

How to Do It:

1) Write just one sentence for each major idea presented in class
2) New main idea? New sentence!
3) Number the sentences, if you find that helpful
4) Organize the sentences by topic, if you find that helpful

Example 1: The Sentence Method

Today's date   Page number
Class/main topic

Sentence Method Overview

1. The sentence method requires that you write **one** sentence for each new thought, fact, person, formula, or topic.
2. Your sentence should explain the thought, fact, person, formula, or topic in a way that you understand.
3. When the professor begins a new thought, begin a new sentence.

Tips for Success

4. Organize the sentences by topic
5. Be concise—don't use ten words when five will do
6. Use **bolding**, underlining, or ALL CAPS to stress key ideas or phrases

Pros & Cons

7. **Pros:** Writing just one sentence helps you focus on the crucial information
8. **Cons:** It can be challenging to summarize complex ideas into one sentence

Example 2: The Sentence Method (Science Class Example)

Today's date   Page number
Class/main topic

The Milky Way Galaxy vs. the Universe

The Milky Way Galaxy[2]

1. The Milky Way galaxy was once thought to comprise the entire universe, but is now understood to be **only one** galaxy in **a universe filled with billions of galaxies.**
2. Our Sun is one of at least **100 billion** stars in the Milky Way.
3. The Milky Way is a **spiral-shaped** galaxy about 100,000 **light-years across.**
4. Thousands of planets (called "exoplanets") are orbiting other stars in our galaxy.

5. When you look up into the night sky, every single star you see has at least one planet orbiting it!

6. At the center of our galaxy is a **supermassive black hole** that has tons of matter packed into a tiny area; it creates a gravitational field so strong nothing can escape, not even light!

The Universe

1. The universe is filled with billions of galaxies, including the one in which our planet (Earth) exists: the Milky Way galaxy.
2. Our universe is **mostly empty space.**
3. The universe is **95% dark energy and dark matter**—the rest (including everything on earth, the planets, and the stars) is the other 5%.
4. About **2/3** of the galaxies scientists have seen are **spiral-shaped** like ours.
5. The rest have oval-like shapes, but a few have weird shapes like tooth-picks or rings!

The Mapping Method

The Mapping Method allows you to create a *graphic*, visual representation of information. It'll help you to see the relationships between the key ideas. We'll look at an example below, but there are many, many ways to do a mapping method, so feel free to get creative!

Example 1: The Mapping Method

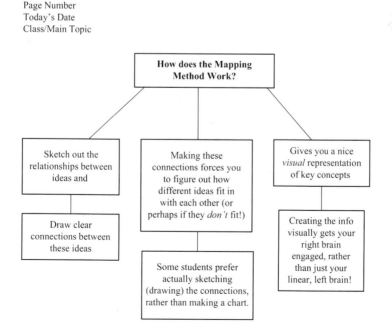

Now that you've seen how to do all five note-taking methods, experiment with creating your own style, using the best elements of each.

Also, keep in mind that the best note-taking method for one class (such as science) might not be the best method in another class (such as math). There's no "right" or "wrong" method here. Just do whatever works for you—and keep practicing! The more you take notes, the better you'll get at it.

How to Use Your Notes

I see it all the time, especially in math classes. Students take diligent, detailed notes in class. Then, when test time rolls around, they can't remember the steps to solving the problems. When I ask them how often they reviewed and studied their notes, their answer is the same: They didn't.

I hope you see their mistake.

It's critical that you **review those notes you worked so hard to take.** Writing down the information once is good, but it's not good enough.

You must read, review, and annotate those notes, and you must do it often. This is how you get the information to sink into your brain and easily recall it when test time rolls around. If you don't review your notes, you won't get the most out of all that hard work you put into making them.

Let's go over how to properly use those notes in three steps:

1) **Read:**
   - **Read your notes before and/or after every single class meeting**
     - Reading the notes soon after you take them helps you find any errors you may have made or gaps you didn't quite fill. When you discover these issues, check with your textbook, classmates, and/or instructor. Then, fix! The last thing you want is to discover your notes are incomplete a day or two before a big test!
2) **Review:**
   - **At the end of each week, review *all notes for the week***
     - By this point, your brain is now receiving the information for the *third* time, which signals that it's important and needs to be stored near the front of the brain for quick and easy retrieval
3) **Annotate:**
   - As you read through your notes, annotate them—meaning, highlight, and/or underline key words, phrases, and ideas
     - You can make text boxes or circle important information, too
     - Draw diagrams or sketch outlines to help you understand
     - Write notes to yourself, or pencil in questions to remind yourself to ask them
   - Interacting with your notes forces your brain to engage with the information and thus process it more deeply
     - The more you engage, the more the information sticks—and the easier it is to recall

Now that you've learned key note-taking principles, the major note-taking systems, and how to use those notes, let's go over a few final tips for note-taking.

Final Tips

- **Get *quality* pens**
  - Cheap pens are cheap for a reason, so don't economize here! You need a quality instrument that won't break on you at key moments
  - Ensure the pens can keep up with your hand as it flies across the page—and without smudging or smearing
  - Try many different types, kinds, and brands of pens
    - *Feel* each pen in your hand as you write. You'll soon be able to tell the difference between one that works for you, and one that doesn't
- **Use colorful pens**
  - Get pens in colors you love
  - Colors send signals to our brain to pay attention, so just making this one change can help take your note-taking to the next level—and you'll probably enjoy it more!
- **Write—don't type—your notes, if at all possible**
  - Research out of UCLA[3] shows that the physical act of writing your notes *by hand* helps you remember the information better than if you'd just typed it
  - If you're not a quick writer, this will be a challenge for you, but remember that you can always request permission to record your professor's lectures. Then, you can pause and/or rewind as needed

Suggested Exercise

1) Choose one of the note-taking methods discussed in this chapter and then find a short lecture, podcast, sermon, talk, or other recorded speech online. Listen to and/or watch this talk while you practice taking notes to it via the note-taking method you chose.
2) Repeat step one—except choose a different note-taking method this time.
3) Repeat step one again—except, again, choose yet another note-taking method that you haven't yet tried.
4) Look over your three sets of notes and study them. Which one do you find easiest to read and understand? Why? How much does the subject or topic impact your understanding vs. the note-taking method? Do you think perhaps one method of note-taking might be best suited for certain classes? Explain.
5) Examine your current pens/pencils for note-taking. Are they working well for you, or should you buy new ones? If you need new ones, take yourself shopping and buy some quality new pens. (Remember, writing instruments are an investment, so don't cheap out here!)

Notes

1 **See these sources for more information:** U.S. Department of Veteran's Affairs:ht tps://va.gov/opa/publications/factsheets/fs_americas_wars.pdf
   Congressional Research Service: U.S. Dept. of Defense: https://defense.gov/ casualty.pdf. https://fas.org/sgp/crs/natsec/RS22926.pdf RAND Army Research Division:https://rand.org/pubs/research_reports/RR1928.html?adbsc=social _20180320_2212921&adbid=975928167633334272&adbpl=tw&adbpr =22545453
2 Source: https://solarsystem.nasa.gov/solar-system/beyond/overview/
3 Read the full article by Mueller here: https://linguistics.ucla.edu/people/hayes/ Teaching/papers/MuellerAndOppenheimer2014OnTakingNotesByHand.pdf

9 Study Smarter, Not Harder

IN THIS CHAPTER, YOU WILL LEARN TO:

• Find your perfect study strategies, places, and times
• Avoid major study blunders so you study smarter, not harder
• Master studying for *any* subject or class

"How can I study successfully?"

This is indeed a critical question to ask in learning to become a top student.

Many "success" books will quickly offer you an answer, too. They'll insist they know the top 100 ways you *must* study or ten things you must *never* do to become a straight-A student. However, the truth is that learning how to study successfully is a **process**, one that you'll refine over time. It's also highly personal to each learner.

No one can tell you, for example, that you must study 2.56 hours for your math class and 1.9 hours for your history test. Perhaps that strategy works for one person, but that doesn't mean it'll work for you. How much to study, when, and how depends on many factors—the most important of which is *you* and how *you* learn.

What works for one student may not work for another. That's why it's so important that you keep *practicing* your studying techniques.

Just like doctors practice medicine, as a student, you'll *practice* the art of studying. The more you practice, the better you'll get. Yet, it is important that you have some guidelines for studying because there are proven strategies that work and many that don't work. If you don't know the differences, you'll probably waste many hours and much precious energy on bad study strategies that will only frustrate you.

Let's begin, then, with some proven study tips to help you maximize your study time, and then we'll go over how you can develop and perfect your own personal study style.

General Studying Tips

Spaced repetition is key

- Review often—**repetition** is key to learning
    - Don't expect to listen to a class lecture *once* and somehow magically remember it weeks later on the test. You won't! The brain needs to hear or see information over and over to commit it to memory. If you're not reviewing, you're not going to remember. Review = Remember!
- Put some time and space between those review sessions
    - Study for an hour or so each day, or every other day (rather than five hours on one day)

Don't cram!

- Study in 45 or 50-minute chunks
- Don't try to cram everything into a six-hour marathon study session. You'll overload your poor brain!
    - If you need six hours total of study time, divide that six hours into an hour per day for six days or two hours per day for three days

Keep up with in-class work

- Keeping up with homework means you're already studying and learning! When "study time" comes, you'll actually just be reviewing, not learning new information
- Do your homework when it's due so you don't fall behind
    - Studying can quickly become a nightmare if you have to study AND complete past-due homework, too
- If you keep up with the homework, your notes will be better, too, because you'll understand the material better, which, in turn, will making studying much, much easier
- Don't let homework fall by the wayside, even if your professor doesn't grade it. Do it on time, and do all of it. If you have questions on it, ask immediately while it's fresh in your brain

Start studying two weeks early

- Plan ahead to start studying for that test two weeks before the exam
- This way, you give yourself plenty of time to learn, review, and test yourself on the information

Test yourself

- How do you know if you truly know the material or not? Don't wait until test day to find out. Create your own test!
- Spend an hour or two making yourself the hardest test you can create. (No simple True/False or multiple choice!)
    - Make yourself define terms and produce answers by recall—*not* just choosing from a list
- Then, use your notes and the textbook to make an answer key. Put the test and answer key away for a day or two. Then, take the test and

grade it. You'll then know if you're ready for the test. If not, review, and then re-test until you ace it

Study in multiple places

- Some students get bored going to the same study place each time, so try changing up where you go. Just keep in mind what places/times work for you, and which don't (we'll cover this in more depth below)
- Move from the library to a cozy café, or vice versa

Don't over study

- Know when to quit. Pay attention to your brain and body. If you're exhausted, staring at the words as they swim on the page before you, you're probably burnt out. It's time to stop!
- Only you will know for certain how long is *too long* for you, but in general, studying in shorter blocks of two to four hours (with breaks in between!) is better than studying for six to eight hours straight.

Take regular breaks

- Give yourself a break in between subjects or on the hour if you're studying for hours at a time
- Get up and walk around. Get something to eat. Make a phone call. Watch some funny videos or a good TV show. Go outside. Hang with your favorite friend or family member. Relax. Then, you can get back to work

Find the best study methods for each subject/class

- What works for English class might not work for science, so adjust your study methods based on the class/subject
  - For example, making flash cards and just memorizing the information might be sufficient prep for a history test. However, in math class, it probably won't be. Instead, you'll probably need to write out the steps to solving, study examples, and practice working them

Review old homework

- If old homework is graded, by all means, review it!
- See if you understand all your errors. If not, go to office hours and/or tutoring

Study old exams and quizzes

- Use any returned class materials to learn your professor's test/quiz style
- What types of questions does she tend to ask?
  - Multiple choice? Essay? Fill-in-the-blank?
- What are her focal points?
  - Philosophical questions? Definitions? Dates?
  - Textbook readings?
  - Diagrams or charts from the textbook?
  - Lecture material? Class discussions?

Study a range of subjects in each study session

- Change things up by studying math for one hour and then switch to English for the next hour, etc.

- This way, you're working multiple parts of the brain and giving other parts a nice respite

Conduct a cumulative (overall) review of class material

- For example, ask yourself:
  - Do I know the key vocabulary?
  - Can I explain who the major thinkers in the field are, their contributions, and why they matter?
  - Do I know major formulas, dates, places, times, or other critical ideas discussed in class or listed on handouts?

Assess your study methods' effectiveness often—and adjust where needed

- Keep a journal of your study methods so you can keep track of what you're doing, when, and how
  - If you ace a test, make a note of how you studied—when, where, how long, what methods, etc.
- Keep using whatever methods work, but adjust when needed

Keep calm and complete one step at a time

- If you feel yourself getting overwhelmed, just do *one step at a time.* Don't think about the next ten things you must do. That will stress you out! Just start with the first item, then move to the next, then the next. Slowly, you'll start making progress
- Remind yourself that you're doing your best. That's all you can do, anyway, so don't listen to the voice of stress. Listen to the voice of calm

Seek help from experts

- If you're struggling in a certain subject, don't suffer in silence! Go to the professor, your teaching assistant, or a student who majors in that subject
  - See if they'll share their tips for studying in that discipline

Now that you have an idea of general study principles, let's dive into how you can figure out the best study methods for you, beginning with the most important: finding your perfect study place and time.

Find Your Perfect Study Place and Time

To get started, begin answering the following questions:

WHERE do you study best?

- Inside or outside?
- Near a window or tucked away in a dark corner?

- At a library?
- In a computer lab?
- In a coffee shop?
- On a sun-drenched patio at a local café?
- At your dining room table?
- In a park, under a tree?

WHEN do you study best?
- Early morning?
- Mid-afternoon?
- Evening?
- Late at night?

WITH WHOM do you study best?
- Alone?
- With one other person?
- With two to three others?
- With a large group?

WITH WHAT do you study best?
- With food?
  - Large meal?
  - Snack?
- With a beverage?
  - Tea?
  - Coffee?
  - Juice?
  - Wine?
- With music?
  - Classical?
  - Jazz?
  - Rock?

WHEN should you review class notes?
- Right before class?
- Just after class?
- After you've had a couple of hours away from your classes?

Once you've answered these questions, it's time to put those answers into action. For example, if you discover your best study place/time is in the morning, outside, on a patio, with a glass of iced tea (this is *my* perfect study place!), then by all means, get up early, head to that patio, and get to work!

Now that you're ready to implement your study place and time, let's find your best study methods and strategies.

Find Your Perfect Study Methods

To discover your optimum study strategies, you'll need to do a bit of research to determine the ways in which you learn best.

You may have heard of the different "types" of learners, such as visual, auditory, and kinesthetic. However, learning is a highly complex endeavor, so don't pigeonhole yourself into *only* one type of strategy. Branch out and see if other methods might work, too. Mix your favorite visual strategies with audio and kinesthetic strategies to customize and strategize your learning. This is especially important to try in classes in which you're struggling. It might simply be that you need some new study methods.

To begin, let's see how you might learn best. Take "What Kind of Learner Am I?" quizzes online—take three or four different quizzes, and then compare the results. I'll list below a few suggested quizzes:

- http://vark-learn.com/the-vark-questionnaire/
- https://webtools.ncsu.edu/learningstyles/
- http://bunbury.wa.gov.au/pdf/environment/u472/Appendix%2019% 20U472%20Community%20Facilitator%20Kolb%20Questionnaire %20Final.pdf
- http://educationplanner.org/students/self-assessments/learning-styles- quiz.shtml

Let's now go over some specific strategies you can try, based on visual, kinesthetic, and auditory principles. Remember, don't limit yourself only to visual strategies if, for example, the quizzes agree you're highly visual. The visual strategies might be your primary ones, but try mixing in some audio and kinesthetic ones that you like, too.

Also, keep this in mind as well: By no means can or should you try *all* of the strategies listed below. There are way too many! Just read over them and see which ones speak to you; then, try those. Keep track of what works and what doesn't, and adjust when needed.

Visual Study Strategies

Take notes on class lectures and the textbook readings
- Most students know they must take notes on class lectures, but you should take notes on your textbook as you read it, too

- Textbooks contain a *huge* amount of complicated information. Explaining this info to yourself via your own notes will help you break it down and better understand it
  - Re-order the material, if you like, so it makes sense to *you*
  - Explain it to yourself, *in your own words*
- Read and re-read these notes often (at least once per week)
- Write down questions you have, and then go ask the professor or TA

Annotate your notes

- Highlight key vocabulary words or important phrases
- Underline critical passages or key vocabulary words
- Make notes to yourself as you review
  - What ideas, questions, or insights occur to you as you re-read?
    - Write these in the margins of your notes in a different color pen

Annotate your textbook

- Just as you annotated your notes, also annotate your textbook
  - If you're worried that marking up your book will hurt the buy-back value of the book at the campus bookstore, it won't. Once you use the book, it's "used," even if you never mark it at all, so you might as well get your money's worth!

Make flash cards

- Color-code them if you like (pink for math, purple for English; or, green for Spanish verbs, blue for Spanish nouns, etc.)
- Put vocabulary words on one side and the definition on the other. Quiz yourself until you get them all correct
- Write *only* key information on the card so your mind can take a mental "picture" of it

Sit at the front of the class so you can see the board clearly

- Write down as much as you can during class
- Study the professor's mannerisms to see what she thinks is important

Use colorful pens

- Take notes with one color; then, when you re-read and make follow-up notes, use a different color

Make or find outlines, idea maps, and other visuals of what you learn

- Some students like to draw diagrams, outlines, or maps to explain the information to themselves
- If class diagrams or charts are confusing, why not re-sketch them so they make sense to you? (Check the new drawing with the professor to make sure the information is still correct)
- Other students search the Internet and find images that help them better understand key class concepts; then, they save those images to their phones or laptops and scroll through them for easy review

Study the diagrams, maps, and other visuals included in your textbook or on class handouts

- Test yourself on these and see if you can recreate them from memory

Make yourself visual reminders
- Use sticky notes or erasable pens to put reminders of key info on your mirrors, refrigerator, phone, or in your car, etc.

Kinesthetic Study Strategies

Take notes—use words and images
- Rewrite information in your own words and/or draw pictures, diagrams, outlines, or other images to help you process the information

Type your handwritten notes into your computer
- Try to reorganize these notes so you're engaging with the information in a new way
- Print these notes and then add further handwritten comments or drawings to enhance them (Remember, these notes are for *you*! They don't need to make sense to anyone else!)

Make outlines, diagrams, and charts
- Get creative here. Use giant poster board, white boards, or whatever materials you enjoy most
- Some students have gone as far as to paint an entire wall in their house with chalkboard paint so they can make diagrams and charts on the wall with colorful chalk!

Make flashcards
- Move them around and create games to play with them
- Put the cards you get correct into one pile, and the ones you miss into another pile. Go back through the missed pile until you have none left. Time yourself and try to beat your best time

Turn verbal information into visual-spatial
- "Translate" what you read into a drawing, sketch, or other visual representation
- Put these away for a few days and then come back to them and see if you can explain them to yourself and/or reproduce them from memory

Walk, dance, or pace while you read/study
- Go for a walk and take your notes or flashcards with you
- Some students like to dance or pace while they read, and something about the movement helps them remember the information

Incorporate multimedia into your studying
- Watch videos, take online quizzes, use apps on your phone, make presentations for yourself (via Google Slides or Microsoft PowerPoint)

Physically touch objects while you study
- Squeeze a stress ball, play with clay, bounce a ball, dance, or do some other physical movements while you study

Auditory Study Strategies

Record class lectures
- Be sure to ask permission first!
- Listen to the lectures *several* times, and take notes while you listen

Explain the material aloud
- Find a friend, fellow student, or family member (or just talk to yourself!) and explain the class's key ideas, topics, and vocabulary
- Imagine you're giving a presentation on the information, and structure the information in a way that makes it easy for you to remember and explain it
- Compare your explanation to your professor's from the recorded class lectures

Go to office hours and discuss key ideas with the professor
- Ask questions and respond to the professor's explanations
- Tell the professor you're working through your understanding of the material and hoped he/she might be willing to listen to your explanations to see if you're on the right track

Make yourself an auditory test
- Write down questions to ask yourself, and then answer them verbally
- Do this alone or with a partner. (Be sure to check your answers!)

Talk it out
- Participate in class discussions; discussing what you're learning helps you get feedback and thus deepens your understanding, so speak up in class!
- Discuss what you're learning in class with friends/family members. Their insights will help you gain greater understanding

Listen to music
- Classical or jazz music are popular choices, since they have no lyrics, but try different types of music and see if they work for you
- (One of my students listens to Christmas music year-long, and she says it's a magic elixir that helps her remember the material!)

Read assignments aloud
- Read the textbook, class handouts, and other materials aloud
- Some students like to make it interesting by acting out the material with funny gestures or goofy voices

Turn the information into music
- Make up a rap or song about crucial class information to help you remember it

Suggested Exercise

1) Write down your answers to the questions posed earlier in this chapter about your perfect study place and time. (When you should study, where, etc.)

2) Using what you learned from step 1 above, grab some study materials and then head to your perfect study place at your perfect study time. Try some of your favorite visual, auditory, or kinesthetic strategies from this chapter (or invent your own, unique strategies!).

3) Repeat step 2 with another batch of material, either from the same class, or try a completely different class.

4) Repeat step 3 with yet another batch of material, either from the same class, or try a completely different class.

5) Keep a journal of how well each study session went, for each type of material or class. What worked? What didn't? Why? What would you change, if anything?

10 Ace Tests and Conquer Test Anxiety

IN THIS CHAPTER, YOU WILL LEARN:

- Ways to overcome testing anxiety
- Questions you *must* ask before studying for and taking tests
- The three-step process to acing tests: before, during, and after the test
- How to use failed tests to become a better student

"I just don't test well."

"I studied for HOURS for that stupid test, and I still bombed it."

"When I have a test, I panic, and the second the instructor passes out the exam, I go blank."

"I have no idea how to study for tests."

"I never know what's going to be on the test, so I study the wrong stuff."

If any of the above quotes sound familiar to you, you're definitely not alone. Thousands of students all over the country fear taking tests. In fact, to many students, the word "test" is a four-letter word—one that inspires worry, frustration, and fear.

If you feel this way, too, you may have **test anxiety**. Students who suffer from test anxiety often struggle to concentrate during exams. They report feeling depressed, and they often experience physical symptoms, such as nausea, headaches, and dizziness.

You probably won't be surprised to learn that students who suffer from test anxiety significantly underestimate their abilities to perform well on exams, and in a self-fulfilling prophecy, their scores on exams reflect their beliefs (Zwettler 2018).

That's the bad news. But, there's good news, too, and here it is: You can absolutely overcome test anxiety. In fact, millions of other students have done just that, so you can, too.

It probably won't happen overnight, but if you follow the steps outlined below, you'll soon start noticing the anxiety lessening, and before you know it, you'll be a pro at taking tests.

Steps to Conquering Test Anxiety

1. **Learn to prepare**

   The simple act of learning how to prepare for a test properly will help ease your anxiety. Stay tuned for more information on this step, as we'll cover it in depth throughout this chapter.

2. **Actually take tests**

   The truth is you'll never get better at test taking unless you actually take tests. If a prospective basketball player never practices playing basketball, will he ever become good enough to win the big game? Similarly, you, too, must *practice* to become good at taking tests.

   Before test day arrives, take some practice tests. Treat these testing sessions like rehearsals or dry runs. Time yourself, if you'll be timed, and do your best to make the practice test as similar to the actual test as possible.

   There are thousands of tests available online or via study apps that you could use. You can and should also design your own test using your class notes, handouts, and textbook.

   The idea here is to desensitize yourself to taking tests—and to do so by beginning in a low-stress environment, when it's just for practice, and no actual grade is on the line. The more you practice testing, the more you'll accustom yourself to taking tests.

3. **Scope out the testing site**

   Knowing what the environment of the test will look and feel like will help calm your fears, so take the time to check out the location of your exams. If you're allowed to go inside the actual room, do it!

4. **Envision yourself succeeding on the test**

   Instead of bringing up mental pictures of yourself bombing the test, use that mental energy instead to imagine yourself succeeding. See yourself being calm, cool, and collected. Envision yourself knowing the answers. Imagine yourself smiling as you take the test and thinking, "I'm totally acing this test!" (Some students even like to say positive affirmations like this out loud, so if that helps, do it!)

5. **Breathe**

   When you start feeling anxious, make yourself stop. Pause for a minute, and take a deep breath. Feel your breath rising and falling in your chest. Be very quiet, and connect to your inner calm. Still your thoughts.

   This deep breathing slows your heart and your mind, and it will help you control the anxious thoughts that attempt to race through your head. Practice breathing every day so that when test day arrives, you're a pro at calming yourself.

6. **Nervousness is normal—and helpful**

   If you feel nervous on test day, don't worry; that's perfectly normal. In fact, those butterflies swirling in your stomach will keep you awake and alert, and they're proof positive that you care, which is a great sign for your grade.

7. **Talk to your anxiety**

   When thoughts arise telling you to panic and freak out, refuse to hear them. Firmly tell them, "No." Then, replace them with positive thoughts. For example, think about all the hard work you've already done in class to prepare. You attended class. You listened closely. You took notes. You read the chapters. You studied. Etc., etc., etc. The more positively you speak to yourself about your abilities and work, the more positively you'll start to feel.

8. **Use any "failures"**

   Almost *every* student has failed a test or two. (I definitely have!) The key here is to **learn** from the experience. Figure out what you did wrong, and then correct the issue. Don't see the failure as "proof" that you're not college material. It's not. Even straight-A students fail sometimes. The difference is that they *learn* from those failures and keep going— they don't use them as a reason to give up, so neither should you.

   Since the best way to overcome test anxiety is to understand how to prepare for the test, let's now cover some general test-taking strategies to beef up your testing knowledge.

   We'll cover a lot of ground here, so know that you certainly don't have to follow *all* of these strategies! Try the ones that resonate most with you. As with studying, test taking is an art, so keep practicing that art, and you'll get better and better.

How to Start Preparing

One of the first—and most important—things you must do to prepare for your tests is to find out as much information about the nature and content of the test as you can. This is why it's important to ask some general questions regarding those upcoming exams. If this information isn't provided to you, then you'll want to visit the professor during office hours and inquire.

I'll list below some suggested questions to help you gain that information, but you'll likely need to cater your questions to each unique class and professor. Some professors won't mind a barrage of questions like these, but others might, so read the professor and see how much information he's willing to share. Just be sure it's clear you're **not** asking to try to gain insider information. You don't want to come across as a shady student who's looking to score the answer key! Instead, convey that you simply want to do your absolute best and be prepared.

Also, remember that if you've already taken an exam or two in this professor's class, looking over an old exam will probably answer many of these questions.

Questions to Ask About Your Exams

What type of exam will it be?
- Multiple choice?
- Fill-in-the-blank?
- Essay?
- True/False?

Is the test computerized or paper-based?
- If it's on paper, do you need to bring a blue book, scantron, or other supplies?

Is the test timed?
- If so, how much time do you get?
- If you have documented accommodations, submit them to the SAS office
  i.   If you're not sure how to do this, research "student accommodations" via your college's website or ask your adviser

When and where will the test be given?
- Don't assume the test is given in the regular classroom during class time. Sometimes, tests are given in testing centers or computer labs, so double check
  i.   Final exams in particular are often given on strange days and at odd times, so triple check your final exam dates and times.
- If you're testing at a testing center or other location, what time(s) are you allowed to take it?

What specific topics will be on the test?
- What chapters, class lectures, supplemental materials, etc.?
- Is it cumulative? (*All* material covered in class, or just certain units?)
- Is there a study guide or review sheet?

Does the test cover only in-class discussion, or textbook readings?
- You can also use prior tests from the class to see what particular types of material your professor tends to put on tests
- Most professors take a bulk of their test material from their lectures, so be sure to take great notes *and review those notes*!

How important are diagrams and charts or other illustrations from the textbook?
- Some professors never put these items on tests, but others do, so check
- The professor may or may not divulge this information, but it doesn't hurt to ask. Just be sure you don't ask about specific diagrams or illustrations but these items in general

What other general advice might the professor offer for studying for tests in her class?
- Sometimes this open-ended question is the best one to ask because the professor might just answer all the above questions for you.

Now that you've hopefully found more information regarding the nature of your test, you're ready to study for it.

Many new college students think that all preparation for testing must happen *before* the test. Once that test begins, there's nothing you can do, or so they think.

While they're right that you must prepare before the test, they're wrong that there's nothing you can do to help yourself during the test, or even after it.

In fact, successful test-taking is a three-step process that includes before, during, and after the test.

Be sure to complete *all three stages* for every test in every class, every semester.

What to Do Before the Test

Successful test prep begins long before you begin studying for the test. To ace your exams, complete your in-class and out-of-class prep:

In-Class Preparation

- Attend **every** class meeting and stay for the entire period
- Take good notes
- Ask questions (before, during, or after class) to ensure your understanding
- Participate in class discussions and activities
- Keep any handouts and other class materials organized, in a place easy to find them
- Make note of any terms, processes, or ideas you don't quite understand—then, ask!
- Pay attention to what the professor emphasizes
  - What does *she* think is important?
    - The more time she spends on a topic, the more important it likely is
    - The more homework or course materials she gives on it, the more important it likely is

Out-of-Class Preparation

Every week:

Visualize yourself acing the test
- If you see yourself excelling before you even take the test, you're prepping your subconscious for success

Review your notes *every* week
- Do **not** wait until it's test time to review—if you're reviewing your notes every week, when test time comes, your overall review will be much, much easier

Follow your best study practices, as outlined in Chapter 9

Visit office hours

- Bring your questions on class lectures or course materials and write down the professor's answers

Go to tutoring, if needed

Keep up with the assigned reading

- Do **not** try to complete all readings right before the test

Create study materials that work for *you*

- Make yourself flashcards and quizzes, etc. (Review Chapter 9 in this book, if need be)

1.5–2 weeks before the test:

If there is a review session for the test, attend!

If the instructor will not make a review for you, make one for yourself

Review all material that will be covered—course readings, handouts, class notes, lectures, etc.

Use flash cards to learn vocabulary, formulas, dates, and other information you need to memorize

Write yourself a checklist of what you need to learn before the exam

Check ratemyprofessor.com to see if former students have advice on what you should study

Take a practice test

- Find one online or via a study app, or ask your professor/TA if they have one

Create your own practice test

- Use your class materials (textbook, notes, handouts, etc.) to create it
- Make it hard—really hard
  - Your test should be as hard, if not harder, than the actual test!
- Ensure it mimics the actual test
  - For example, if you must fill in a blank map on the test, print out a blank map, and make yourself fill it in. Then, look over it and see how you did. Study any mistakes you made, then put it away, sleep on it, and try it again the next day. Repeat until you've mastered it
  - Even if you're taking a multiple choice test, don't give yourself easy choices. Make it challenging. Enlist others' help if need be
- If the actual test will be timed, then time yourself
- Grade your test. (Go to the professor if you're not sure about your accuracy)
- You'll get an excellent idea of whether you're ready for the test yet or not. If not, review, and then take the test again and again, until you're ready

Pretend you're the instructor and explain key class concepts and define vocabulary words, etc.

- Talk aloud to yourself or to a friend. (Either way, you'll quickly see what you know, and what you don't!)
- If you're more visual, write it all out, then read over it to check your accuracy

Look back over your homework and re-work any problems you missed to ensure you can now work them correctly

If you work well in groups, form a study group

Visualize yourself doing well on the test and say out loud, "I am going to ace this test!"

The day before the test:

- Do a final review of all material
- Set your alarm(s) to ensure you don't sleep through the test
- Gas up the car or verify other transportation (updated bus pass, etc.)
- Get a good night's sleep
- Eat a light, healthy meal for dinner
  - No heavy, fried foods or anything that might keep you up late
- Avoid caffeine at least three hours before bedtime
- Visualize yourself succeeding on the test
- Pack your bag to ensure you have all materials you need
  - Have your #2 pencil, scantron, pen, calculator, Bluebook, student ID, etc.

Test day—just before the test begins:

- Leave half an hour earlier than usual
- Eat a trusted, healthy meal an hour or two before the test
  - No new, experimental food!
  - Stick to trusted, tried-and-true meals your body has easily digested in the past
- Use the restroom **before** the test
- Show up early so you're not stressing over being late
- If you have time, refresh your memory on anything that's got you worried
- Sit in the seat/place where you feel most comfortable
- Get any materials (pencil, scantron, etc.) ready
- Give yourself a pep talk, and envision yourself succeeding!

What to Do During the Test

Pause.
- If you start panicking, take a break and breathe. Slow down.
- Remind yourself that you've prepared and that you're going to do your best. That's all you can do, anyway, so just keep going the best you

can. If you don't do well, you can cross that bridge when you get there. (We'll discuss options below.)

Read the instructions *first*
- Must you answer **all** questions?
- Or do the instructions say, "Answer 1, 2, 3, or 4"?
  - If you answer all four instead of just one, you will probably lose points for two reasons: 1). You didn't follow instructions, and 2). You didn't develop your answer fully enough.

If you have questions about the test's instructions or wording, don't be afraid to ask

Be sure you have the entire test
- If it's supposed to be 20 questions, be sure you have all 20

Pay close attention to question wording
- Sometimes, tests questions will ask something such as, "Which of the following does *not* equal…" or "Which of the below are **not** true?"

Scan the test and **answer the easiest items first** to build your confidence

If you had to memorize definitions, formulas, or other information, do a "dump" immediately by writing it all down on your exam (if you are allowed)

Answer all questions
- If you don't answer it, then you can't possibly get it right

If you don't know the answer, guess
- For multiple choice, eliminate any answers that are obviously wrong; make your best guess between the remaining options

If it's a timed test, be balanced in checking the clock
- Keep an eye on the clock and budget your time wisely, but don't look at it too much (looking two to three times per hour is plenty)

For true and false questions:
- **Look for <u>absolute</u> qualifiers,** such as Always, All, Never, Nearly, Every, None
  - These usually indicate the answer is **false**
- **Look for <u>relative</u> qualifiers,** such as Occasionally, Often, Sometimes, Frequently, or Seldomly
  - These often indicate the answer is **true**
- If **any** part of the statement/question is false, then the entire answer is false
- For the answer to be true, the entire statement must be true
- If you're not sure, guess. You have a 50/50 chance.

For matching questions:
- Read directions carefully
  - May you use an item more than once?
  - If not, check off each item you use to eliminate them from your choices
- Do the matches you know first

- If you don't know the correct matches, guess by using process of elimination

For multiple choice questions:
- Read the question first
  - Try to answer it *without* looking at the choices
  - Once you think you know the answer, look at the choices
- Read all answer choices before selecting your answer
  - Even if you think you know the answer is "a," **read all choices** to ensure they are all wrong before making your final selection
  - If you think both "a" and "c" are ok, choose which one is the *best* answer
- If it's a scantron test, be sure all bubbles are clearly marked and errors erased

Check your answers before turning in the test
- Do a final quality-check read-through. Ensure you:
  - Still agree with your choices (Don't change an answer unless you are *certain* it's incorrect!)
  - Followed the instructions
  - Answered **all** questions
  - Didn't skip any questions or get off on numbering
  - Put your name and student ID number on the test

What to Do After the Test

Congratulate yourself for taking the test!
- Regardless of your score, just showing up to take a test is an impressive victory!

When you get the test back, **review it**
- **Do not** just look at your grade and toss the paper aside!
  - If you do, how will you learn from the questions missed?
  - It's not just a matter of learning the correct answer, but learning *why* you missed it so you can use that knowledge on future tests and in future classes
- Read over the entire test and your answers—*both* the correct and incorrect
- Look up the incorrect answers to be sure you understand them
- If it's a math test, re-work the problems until you understand them

Go to office hours and ask the professor about any questions you have
- If you don't understand why your answer was incorrect, go to office hours and politely ask
- Sometimes, if you can defend/explain your reasoning for a certain "wrong" answer, the professor may give you a few extra points. (This is up to her, of course, though, so don't expect it!)

If you're allowed to keep the exam, then definitely keep it!

- Study it before your next exam to remind yourself of this instructor's testing style

Make notes on your studying methods

- If you got an "A," then your study methods were successful, and you should keep using them!
- If you did not do as well as you hoped, adjust study methods and/or try new ones

Talk to other students and find out who got an "A"

- See if they'll share their study secrets; usually, they will!

What If You Don't Do Well on the Test??

If you don't do well on a test, don't throw in the towel. Instead, learn from your mistakes by asking yourself some questions:

Did you over study or under study?

- Most students assume when they fail a test that they didn't study long enough. Sometimes, this is true, but sometimes it's not. It is possible to over study and overwhelm your brain. So, pay attention when you're studying. When your brain shuts down and says it's done, listen to it. You can pick up the studying later.
- At the same time, be sure you're giving the material plenty of time to soak into your brain. If you didn't review your notes and studied only one hour for a big test, there's your problem.

Did you review the correct materials?

- Sometimes, the problem is simply that the student didn't review the correct chapters, or he forgot to review the charts or diagrams in the textbook. Make a note of any material covered on the test that you didn't review.
  - Where were any items you missed? Were·they on class handouts? In class lectures? In the textbook?
  - Make a note, so you don't make the same mistake on the next exam.

Did you employ your best study strategies—including time and place?

- If you learn best in a quiet, controlled environment but you studied for this test with three kids racing around you screaming while the dog barked and your phone was blowing up with texts, there's your problem. Next time, go to the library. Or, perhaps the reverse is true. Maybe you hate the library. Fine. Go to a café or study somewhere that you actually enjoy spending time.

Other strategies to try if you don't do well on a test:

- **Ask if you can re-take the test**
  - The answer is probably "no," but if you have extenuating circumstances, he might just let you.

- Ask **if you can do extra credit work**
  - Even just a few points here and there can add up
- **Ask the professor if he would consider dropping your lowest test grade**
  - If you can show significant improvement on the remaining tests, perhaps he might give your lowest-scoring test less weight in your overall grade?

The good news with test-taking is that you'll get better with practice, so keep honing your best test-taking methods, and *don't give up.* Testing can be difficult, but the more you do it, the better you'll get, so keep practicing.

Suggested Exercise

1) Do you feel you have testing anxiety? If so, write about why you think tests make you so anxious.
2) Describe what happens when you begin to test or think about testing. Be honest here, and feel free to recycle, rip up, burn, or otherwise destroy your writing afterwards if you fear anyone reading it!
3) Brainstorm some ideas that you could try that will help you become a calmer test taker. (Feel free to use the ideas suggested here or think of/research your own.)
4) Take some material from your favorite class and make yourself a test on the material.
5) If you haven't already, make an answer key for that test, too, so you can grade the test.
6) Set the test and answer key aside for a day or two and study for the test.
7) When you're ready, take your test. Be sure to create a testing environment as close to the one you'll face in class as possible.
8) Grade your test. (Get help from the professor or TA, if need be.)
9) Make a note of your study methods, test-writing strategies, and overall performance here. How could you do better in the future, or have you found your ideal test-creating and test-taking methods?
10) Repeat as needed with other classes.

11 Understand—and Master—College Technology

IN THIS CHAPTER, YOU WILL LEARN:

- The top "tech" skills you must acquire for success in college
- The chief tech tools to learn for college
- The best, most helpful "tech" recommended by current college students

You probably already know how important it is to develop a solid foundation in using college technology. The better you are at managing college technology, the better your overall experience in college will be—and the less stressful!

Gaining a better understanding of technology will also help make you more marketable to employers, too, as almost all professional jobs now require strong technology skills.

Although learning these new technologies can be frustrating at first, if you keep practicing and ask for help when you need it, your skills will improve, and so will your confidence.

We'll go over in this chapter two areas of technology: skills and tools. Let's begin with the skills you'll need, since these skills will help you with learning the tools.

Tech Skill #1: Learn to Type

There's just no getting around it: You absolutely must learn how to type properly—meaning, *without* looking at the keyboard!

You'll be typing many, many papers in your academic career, and sometimes, these papers will be written during class (when you are timed). If you're hunting and pecking for every letter, it's going to be a nightmare. Writing is hard enough; don't make it harder by not knowing where the letters are located on the keyboard!

With typing, both speed and accuracy count, so even if you already know how to type, work on getting faster and more accurate. The faster you can type, the faster the ideas in your head will be allowed to flow, so invest the time now in learning to type, and it will pay off bountifully in the future.

How to learn:

1) **Take an in-person typing class**
   Your college or university, local library, or community center may offer these classes (sometimes, for free!). Some organizations call these classes "keyboarding" or something similar (rather than "typing"), so look into it and enroll right away.

2) **Take online typing tests**
   If you'd rather practice on your own, go to Google and type in "typing test," and you'll see a plethora of options pop up. Practice a few minutes per day, *every day* until you get better. Keep working until you get up to at least 40 words per minute (the average of most college students).

3) **Watch typing videos online**
   YouTube is filled with various videos aimed at teaching you how to type, so take advantage of the kindness of these creators and learn from them. (If you like their video, pay them back by "liking" it and/or subscribing to their channel.)

Tech Skill #2: Protect Your Privacy and Safety Online

The Internet is the new dark alley, filled with hidden dangers. Pirates and thieves lurk around almost every corner, so be careful when on the Internet! The following tips will help ensure you protect yourself and others while online:

- **Invest in good antivirus software—and keep it updated**
  This software will protect your computer from viruses and malware. You can probably find one for around $50—$100 at Best Buy or other tech-friendly stores. According to PC Mag[1], these are the best:
  - McAfee
  - Norton
  - Trend

Be sure you **never** go online without these protections in place, and check them frequently to be sure they are updated. Some software programs will update for you automatically each day, but if not, check to see if there is an update available before you go online—especially if you're checking your bank account or doing other private transactions!

If you have no idea how to install antivirus software, call the number on the box, and they can walk you through the process, or better yet, if you're buying a new computer, the store where you purchase the computer likely will help you do it.

- **Keep your computer updated**

Be sure your computer's operating system and Internet browsers are up to date. The latest, most up-to-date software will offer you further protection against viruses and other threats, so take the few minutes needed to let your computer update. It can be irritating to have to wait for the computer to update when you just want to get your work done, but getting a virus will be even *more* irritating, so it's worth waiting a minute or two for the protection to kick into place.

To make this easier, turn on your computer's auto update feature. Check the Apple website for the most up-to-date instructions for Mac and the Windows website for PC computers.

- **Check your bank account and credit card statements frequently**

The last thing you need in college is to be dealing with credit card fraud or stolen bank funds! So, be sure you check your account statements often, and if you see anything suspicious, report and dispute immediately. Most credit card companies will investigate for you, and if the charges are fraudulent, they'll refund your money. Banks, on the other hand, are a different matter altogether. For this reason, I would recommend you *avoid* using your bank/debit card for online shopping because these cards rarely carry the same protections that actual credit cards do.

In fact, some debit cards are not protected *at all* against theft or fraud.

Check the terms of your debit card and only shop with credit cards that are 100% protected against theft and fraud. (Also, just FYI, some financial experts suggest you not use your debit card at ATMs or gas pumps, either, since these can be vulnerable to "swiping" schemes, especially during the holiday season.)

- **Shop only on secure sites**

Don't check your bank balance on public computers or even on your phone's Wi-Fi at the local café or while standing in line at the grocery store. You also want to avoid shady websites that don't offer you a secure connection. Before purchasing, verify that the site's URL begins with https:// (that final "s" means secure, and most sites offer a lock sign 🔒).

- **Vary your passwords and change them often**

    Have different passwords for each account. This way, if a hacker gets one password, he can't use it to open all your accounts. If you have trouble keeping track of all your passwords, get a password book, and write password *hints* in it so that you know what the passwords are, but if someone found your book, they wouldn't have all your passwords.

- **Be wise about posting online**

    Do you personally know every single friend or follower you have on Facebook or Instagram? Few people do. Your friends and your friends' friends don't know all of their "friends," either. This means that potentially thousands of people could be seeing your posts that your friends have "liked" or shared.

    Who cares?

    Thieves do.

    They know that we don't know all of our friends and followers, so they purposefully make fake accounts to look for "marks" or targets.

Consider an example: If I post my "I'm in Hawaii!" pictures while I'm in Hawaii, my friends will probably "like" these and comment on them. This seems innocent enough, but actually what I've done is just rolled out the red carpet for thieves to rob my house. I've essentially said, "Hey, thieves?! I'm thousands of miles away; why don't you go rob my house while I'm gone?!"

If you think there's no way a thief could possibly find your house from your Facebook or Instagram account, think again.

According to an NBC news report[2], 500 convicted burglars in New York and New Jersey admitted they used social media to case targets for break-ins. Similarly, in California, a thief used GPS data embedded in photos posted to Facebook and Instagram to get into people's homes. Once he had an address, he stole more than $250,000 in electronics and jewelry along with various other items. In fact, police across the country have been warning residents to be careful what they post to social media.

My point here is this: Thieves can be smart, so don't underestimate them.

Instead, be safe, and keep any clues that you're not at home off the site until you're back, and be sure to use past tense when you speak of vacations, so it's clear you're now home. (For example, "Hawaii *was* so much fun!)

Also, don't post pictures of or talk about your expensive jewelry, televisions, computers, Christmas gifts, etc. Christmas is an especially busy time for thieves, so think twice before posting pictures of that beautiful Christmas tree loaded down with gifts. Even if the gifts aren't expensive, thieves don't know that.

Tech Skill #3: Protect Your Work by Backing It Up

If you're writing an essay or typing out a review for yourself, you certainly don't want to lose all the work you've done, so save that work frequently. Then, once you're finished, back it up by saving it in the cloud, onto a USB drive, or on an external hard drive.

If you're working on a public computer in the computer lab or at the library, don't just save it to that particular computer. How do you know it will still be there when you return? Email it to yourself or save it onto that USB drive.

Tech Skill #4: Understand Keyboard Shortcuts

Keyboard shortcuts allow you to use one or a few keys to perform the operations of the mouse. These shortcuts can save you hours, so it's worth the time to learn to use them.

The tables on the pages below contain the most common keyboard shortcuts, for both PCs and Macs. (I've bolded the ones that are, in my opinion, most helpful for college students, but I encourage you to do your own research, too, and find out which shortcuts you most need to learn.)

Computer Shortcuts for Windows PCs[3]

Press this key	*To do this*
Ctrl + C (or Ctrl + Insert)	**Copy the selected item**
Ctrl + X	Cut the selected item
Ctrl + V (or Shift + Insert)	**Paste the selected item**
Ctrl + Z	Undo an action
Alt + Tab	Switch between open apps
Alt + F4	Close the active item, or exit the active app
Windows logo key + L	Lock your PC or switch accounts
Windows logo key + D	Display and hide the desktop
Ctrl + F4	Close the active document (in apps that are full-screen and allow you to have multiple documents open simultaneously)
Ctrl + A	**Select all items in a document or window**
Ctrl + R (or F5)	Refresh the active window
Ctrl + X	Cut the selected item
Ctrl + Y	Redo an action
Ctrl + Z	Undo an action

(*Continued*)

(*Continued*)

Press this key	To do this
Ctrl + plus (+) or Ctrl + minus (−)	Zoom in or out of a large number of items, like apps pinned to the Start screen
Ctrl + mouse scroll wheel	Change the size of desktop icons or zoom in or out of a large number of items, like apps pinned to the Start screen
Ctrl + Right arrow	Move the cursor to the beginning of the next word
Ctrl + Left arrow	Move the cursor to the beginning of the previous word
Ctrl + Down arrow	Move the cursor to the beginning of the next paragraph
Ctrl + Up arrow	Move the cursor to the beginning of the previous paragraph

---

KEYBOARD SHORTCUTS FOR MAC[4]

- **Command-B:** Bold the selected material
- **Command-C:** Copy the selected item to the Clipboard. This also works for files in the Finder
- **Command-U:** Underline the selected material
- **Command-V:** Paste the contents of the Clipboard into the current document or app. This also works for files in the Finder
- **Command-A:** Select all items
- **Command-F:** Find items in a document or open a Find window
- **Command-G:** Find again: Find the next occurrence of the item previously found. To find the previous occurrence, press Shift-Command-G
- **Command-H:** Hide the windows of the front app. To view the front app but hide all other apps, press Option-Command-H
- **Command-P: Print the current document**
- **Command-S: Save the current document**
- **Command-T:** Open a new tab
- Option-Command-Esc: force quit an app

Tech Skill #5: Know Microsoft Office Basics

You probably already know you must learn to navigate word processing programs like Microsoft Word, but do you also know you should learn to use Power Point and Excel, too? (These three programs are considered the "Microsoft Office Suite.")

Mastering the Microsoft Office Suite will make you an invaluable employee after graduation, not to mention it will make your college days much, much easier. Learning to use these programs will also help you learn to navigate the Google Drive as well because their products use almost identical commands.

Set aside a little bit of time each week to work on learning these programs. Some students like to learn hands-on by simply opening the programs and tinkering around. Other students have no idea where to even begin, so they prefer watching YouTube videos or buying a well-written guide to help them. Do whatever works for you, but try to be consistent. The programs take a little getting used to initially, but be patient with yourself, and keep at it. Seek help when you need it.

Also, check into classes in your community. Most libraries and community centers offer free classes where you can learn to use these programs, or you can also ask your adviser if your school has an official class you could take. (Perhaps even for college credit!)

Tech Skill #6: Know How to Conduct Online, Academic Research

Many new college students think that "online research" means going to Google and "typing in stuff." Yet, that type of simple search is an Internet search, *not* academic research.

To conduct collegiate-level research, you'll need to research your topic via **academic databases and journals**, which include only scholarly work.

Usually, you can find these academic sources through your college's library website. If you're not sure how to access these, visit the library and ask for a research librarian, or if your school's library offers online chat help (most schools do!), then seek their help. Don't feel like you're bothering them, either, because you're not. It's their job to help you. Besides, most librarians are happy to assist you and look forward to getting to work with students. (After all, this is why they became research librarians at a college or university—to help students!)

Now that you've gained an understanding of the tech skills to acquire, let's cover some of the technology tools that can help you become a better student.

Technology Tools to Learn

You'll quickly discover as you move through your college classes that some professors embrace technology, and others do not. However, even if your professors aren't exactly tech savvy, that doesn't mean you have to stay in the dark ages with them! The plethora of online study tools is practically infinite, so you can use these tools to customize your learning and become a better student.

We'll divide these technologies into two categories: In-class tech and out-of-class tech.

In-Class Technologies

- **Learning Management Systems (L.M.S.)**

    Learning management systems are essentially online classrooms, somewhat similar to Facebook, but for educational purposes. These systems provide an online platform that allows your professor to communicate with you, and vice versa. Many professors post announcements, assignments, grades, and course documents via these learning management systems, and you may turn in assignments exclusively through them. Examples of L.M.S. include:
    - Blackboard
    - TRACS
    - Google Classroom
    - Schoology
    - Brightspace
    - Canvas
    - Moodle

    If you take an online class, your entire interaction with your instructor and classmates might be conducted via an online learning management system.

If you plan to take an online class or even a hybrid class (part online, part in-person), find out which LMS your school uses and learn to use it as best you can. See if your college has tutorials and/or videos that teach you the basic functions.

Learning these skills ahead of time will save you stress and worry in the long run. Think about, for example, how stressful it might be if you realize you have only an hour to post a thread on your class's Discussion Board via Blackboard, and you don't even know how to find and log into Blackboard, let alone how to post on the discussion board!

Luckily, most of these systems have similar features and functions, so if you learn to navigate the most common ones, it will help immensely. Let's go over them briefly:

- **Announcements:**
    - Professors may post announcements for students to read. These can be found under the announcement tab
        - Check your announcements page often, preferably two to three times per week, but at least once per week to make sure you have

not missed any important announcements (such as due date changes, cancelled classes, new homework assignments, etc.)

- **Discussion board**
  - This feature allows students and professors to create a discussion thread and reply to others' threads
  - Many professors in English, philosophy, psychology, history, and sociology classes will use this feature to have students post their thoughts on homework, class readings, and/or class discussions to keep the dialogue going
  - Students can also post questions of their own to solicit feedback from other students and/or the instructor about assignments or other aspects of the class
- **Email**
  - Students and professors can send mail to one another via this feature
  - Students can also email other students, including their entire class!
    - This is a great way to solicit help from other students, form study groups, and/or get missed notes or assignments
- **Course content**
  - Some instructors will post assignments, course documents, videos, links, and other resources
    - Check under the course content for extra copies of the course syllabus, course calendar, or other assignments (such as essay prompts, exam reviews, or slide notes, etc.)
- **Google Drive ("The Drive")**
  - The Google Drive is an online file storage service available to Gmail users. The Drive allows users to store and share files of many types:
    - **Word processing** documents (called Google Docs), similar to Microsoft Word documents
    - **Spreadsheet** documents (called Google Sheets), similar to Microsoft Excel documents
    - **Slideshow** documents (called Google Slides), similar to Microsoft Power Point documents

The great innovation with the Google Drive is that you can share your documents with others, and they can share their documents with you. So, for example, in your English class, you can compose your essay on the Drive as a Google Doc, and share with your instructor. She can then comment on your essay right there in the Drive, and you never have to print anything!

Just be sure to check with your instructors about how they'd like to receive documents from you. Some instructors love the Drive; others do not!

Another great aspect of the Google Drive is that files are automatically saved, and you can access your documents anywhere in the world—so long as you have Internet access and are logged into your Google Account!

Top Tech Recommended by Current College Students

I polled my students over the course of several semesters about their favorite apps, the ones they found the most helpful as students. Here are their recommendations:

- Quizlet

    Quizlet is an online (both mobile and web-based) study application. It allows students to study via flashcards, games, quizzes, and other tests.

    When using Quizlet, you can log in and choose which study concepts to review. These concepts can be created by the actual instructor, generated by other users, or created by you yourself.

Pros of Quizlet:

- It's easy to use and free (although, you can upgrade to their fee service)
- It's highly flexible; use Quizlet for virtually any class type or level
- It's great for classes with high memorization needs
- You can create quizzes and games to test yourself
- It features different question types
    - Multiple-choice, true/false, matching, etc.
- It's "smart"
    - It increases or decreases the difficulty of questions based on your performance

Cons of Quizlet:

- If you rely on other users' cards, you're risking quality and accuracy
    - How do you know for certain the information is accurate?
- If you create your own, it can be time consuming

- Scanner Pro

    With this app, you can turn your tablet or phone into a portable scanner. For a one-time fee (check the website for the most current prices), you can scan important documents right into your phone or tablet. For example, many students like to scan textbook pages or exam reviews so they'll have these pages with them anytime they need them (rather than carrying around a heavy textbook or bulky binder).

- Exam Countdown Lite

    If you aren't sure when your next essay is due or the date of that pesky math mid-term, open up your Exam Countdown Lite app and it counts it down for you—how many weeks, days, and even minutes!

The app also allows you to color-code different types of assignments or different classes, or you can customize your icons for each subject.

Many students have told me this app is a lot of work upfront because you have to enter *all* of your assignments into it, but once you've done the leg work, it's easy to use because you simply open it and check to see what's due.

- **Dragon Anywhere**

This voice dictation software allows you to transcribe your thoughts, notes, or ideas right into your computer, tablet, or phone! If you're an auditory learner, this could be a great app for you. Rather than writing or typing everything, you can simply turn on the Dragon Anywhere recording, speak your thoughts aloud, and it transcribes them for you.

Pros of Dragon Anywhere

- Fixing mistakes is pretty easy; simply say "delete"
- The more you use it, the more accurate it becomes
- Allows you to focus on your ideas, not on perfect grammar, spelling, and punctuation and/or typing
- Great for students with carpal tunnel syndrome or other issues with hands/fingers
- Great for visually challenged students

Cons of Dragon Anywhere

- It's not free (check their website for current pricing)
- It may take a bit of working to learn to use it (but remember, all technology has a learning curve)
- It won't understand what you're saying 100% of the time, and that can be frustrating

All of the recommendations in this chapter are just that, so be sure to do your own research to see what tech tools and skills *you* need, not just for your particular school but for your major and future career as well. The more you start acquiring those skills now, the more refined they'll be by the time you graduate.

Suggested Exercise

1) Choose one of the college technologies we covered in this chapter (such as Blackboard or Google Classroom, etc.). Write out a plan for how you can master the basics of it in the next month.
2) Choose one of the recommended apps (such as Quizlet or Dragon Anywhere), and try it out for the next few weeks.

3) Go buy an external hard drive, USB drive, or Cloud Account, and save your most important documents onto it.

4) Take an online typing test and see what your current typing speed is. (Take two or three to get the most accurate results!) Then, spend at least an hour over the next two weeks practicing typing, and take the test again. Record your new speed. Repeat the process over the next few months. See how fast—and accurate—you can become at typing.

Notes

1 See Mr. Rubenking's full recommendations here: https://pcmag.com/roundup/256703/the-best-antivirus-protection for more information and a detailed chart.

2 Read the full story here: https://nbcnewyork.com/news/local/Investigations-I-Team-Social-Media-Use-Survey-New-York-New-Jersey-390938211.html

3 Source: https://support.microsoft.com/en-us/help/12445/windows-keyboard-shortcuts

4 Source: https://support.apple.com/en-us/HT201236

12 Where to Find Help

**IN THIS CHAPTER, YOU WILL LEARN WHERE
TO FIND HELP WITH ISSUES SUCH AS:**

- Emergency financial assistance for tuition and/or books
- Disability Services
- Legal or medical issues
- Computer and other technology problems
- Harassment or other unethical behaviors you encounter at college

---

Most of us don't like to ask for help, but it's crucial that we do. In fact, asking for help is not a sign of weakness or stupidity. It's the exact opposite: It's a sign of intelligence and strength. It shows that you know what you don't yet know, and that is wise indeed.

In this chapter, we'll cover some of the most frequently encountered issues students face in college. If you don't find your particular issue on the list, see the chart at the end of the chapter as a general reference for suggestions of places to go for help.

Since financial concerns are often the most pressing for many students, let's begin with those types of issues and where you can go for help with them.

Financial Issues

If You Can't Pay Your Tuition
Almost all of us have struggled with that tuition bill at least once. Yet, before you jump to dropping out of school because you can't make your payment, try these options first:

Student Emergency Fund

- Many colleges and universities have an emergency fund for students in need
    - Yet, few students know about these types of funds, so often the money sits there, unused
    - Inquire with your adviser, dean, or counselor, and see if your school has such a fund and how you might qualify
- Get all your paperwork together (pay stubs, W2 forms, hospital records, etc.) to prove your need

Free Textbook Programs

- Many schools have special programs that offer free access to textbooks
    - Often, these programs are unadvertised, so check with your dean, counselor, adviser, and/or financial aid office to inquire

Financial Aid Office Assistance

- Go to your financial aid office and share the details of your issue. How much were you awarded? How much more do you need?
- The financial aid office might be able to increase your award or point you to other monetary sources (school-specific scholarships, grants, internships, residencies, fellowships, etc.)

Make an Appeal

- If your financial aid award wasn't big enough to cover your school expenses, you can appeal, especially if important changes have occurred in your financial situation. Contact the financial aid office to see where you should send your appeal letter
- In the letter, explain your situation honestly and clearly. Outline what happened (you lost your job, your spouse was laid off, your child or parent got sick, etc.). Be sure your include proof of these situations to accompany your request

Payment Plans

- Most schools offer tuition payment plans whereby you pay in installments. Check your Bursar's or Student Services office to inquire
- If you are awarded a payment plan, make absolutely certain you pay before the deadline so you don't get dropped from your classes

Crowdfunding

- Crowdfunding sites allow your neighbors, friends, family, coworkers, and even random kind-hearted strangers to help you make that tuition payment
- Check out GoFundMe, Indiegogo, Kickstarter, Patreon, or YouCaring, and see if you can raise those funds

If You Need Transportation to Class

Many colleges and universities offer free passes for local public transit (buses and trains). Some schools even offer free shuttles and campus escort services to make sure you not only have a ride but that you make it to that ride safely.

If You Need Food

Many schools have food pantries that offer students a selection of free healthy foods. Check your school's website or ask a friendly adviser or dean about what options your school offers.

Also, check at your school's Student Life Office. They almost always have free coffee, donuts, pizza, candy, and/or other goodies.

Academic-Related Issues

If You Need to Leave Your Classes Before the End of the Semester:

Many students think if they just stop going to class and turning in work, then the professor will drop them. This is *not* necessarily the case! The professor may or may not drop you.

It's not their responsibility to drop you. It's yours.

If you absolutely cannot finish your classes (due to illness, a death in the family, etc.), be sure you **officially** drop your classes—meaning that you withdraw from them with the full knowledge and consent of your school.

- Most colleges will allow you to drop classes via your online student services menu with the click of a few keys
- Other schools are stricter and require students to get professors' signatures before the drop is official. Double check with your institution to see what the policy is

It's critical you follow your school's official process for dropping

When you officially drop by the proper deadlines, you'll simply receive a "W" (Withdrawal), which will not affect your G.P.A. (However, it may affect your financial aid award.)

If you just stop attending your classes and not turning in assignments, you'll probably receive an "F," which will absolutely impact your G.P.A.—and your financial aid.

If Your Professor Behaves in Unfair and/or Unethical Ways:

Happily, this issue rarely occurs. Most professors are helpful and kind, but occasionally students run into a jerk professor who's mad at the world and takes it out on his/her students.

If it does happen to you, here's what you do:

Step One: Always go to the professor first and try to work it out with him/her

- Even if you know it's not going to do any good, do it anyway
- Be polite and respectful to them, no matter how they treat you
- Keep track of all communication with the professor

Step Two: If the professor is not helpful, then go to the Department Chair

- You should be able to find this email address via the college's directory
- Send him/her an email requesting an appointment to discuss your class (Give them the course number and your instructor's name)
- Mention that you already spoke with the instructor
- Bring all your documentation with you to the meeting. Be professional and polite; don't call the instructor names. Just stick to the facts
- If you have an outcome in mind (such as raising your grade from a C to a B), then state this goal, and then give supporting evidence

Step Three: If the Department chair is not helpful, go to the Dean of Students

- Follow the steps outlined above

Step Four: If the Dean is not helpful, go to his/her supervisor

- Follow the instructions above

Be sure you follow the chain of command.

If you don't, then you've given college leadership an excuse to dismiss you and your complaint. However, when you follow the proper procedures, no matter how irritating they might be, you're much more likely to be heard and have the situation resolved.

If You Need Help with Documenting Your Disability—or To Verify You Have One

Go to the Student Disability Office, also often called "The Office of Student Disability Service" or "Student Accessibility Services."

They will assist you with getting documentation for your disability and help ensure any doctor-recommended accommodations are honored for the life of your academic career at that college or university.

Accommodations vary based on the particular type of disability, but they can include:

- Increased time on tests
- Getting a reader
- Receiving materials in alternate format (such as transcribed audio)
- Special reading software
- Alternative test locations
- Permission to take breaks during test
- Food/drinks allowed in class

If You Want to Meet Other Students and Get Involved on Campus

Check out your college's Student Life Center. They will usually provide students with a low-stress place to hang out and meet other students. They also often have free food and other schwag (t-shirts, pens/pencils, calendars, and other random student fare) for students, and they'll have a definitive guide on student news, events, organizations, and activities.

If You Want to Study Abroad

If you are interested in spending a semester, or even a year, abroad, visit your school's Study Abroad Center. Most schools offer programs in which you can go abroad (to Spain, Mexico, Egypt, Italy, England, Costa Rica, etc.) *while* you earn college credit!

If You Need Help with Research for a Paper

Libraries are not only well stocked with books. They also have millions of digital resources filled with academia-approved sources (much better than Google!). Check with your library for information on how to access your school's e-books, journals, and other periodicals. If you're not the best researcher in the world, no worries; research librarians are there to help you.

If You Need Tutoring

Don't hire a private tutor before checking to see if your school offers free tutoring on campus. Most do.

They're often called "Learning Labs," "Student Learning Assistance Centers," or "Academic Success Centers."

Many colleges also offer a writing-specific tutoring center called The Writing Center, where you can receive one-on-one assistance with writing essays or other English-class related topics.

Technology Issues

If You Need Help with Your Computer

Many colleges and universities now have technology services and/or technology stores to support students with issues such as purchasing laptops, downloading virus protection, and staving off ransom ware. Many of these centers offer discounts for students and are cheaper compared to other technology stores and services.

If You Need a Computer or Tablet

Visit the library and/or computer lab on your campus. Most likely, you can either use a computer or tablet on campus or even check one out and take it with you, sometimes for the entire semester.

If You Need Internet at Home

1. **Check out the FCC's Program Lifeline**
   a. It provides low-cost Internet for eligible subscribers
   b. To see if you qualify, visit https://www.lifelinesupport.org/
2. **Check with your local Internet provider**
   a. Some Internet providers offer low-cost services to qualified individuals

---

Personal Issues

If You Need Medical Services

Most universities have a student health center that offers free services to students. Here, you can receive general health advice, birth control, flu shots, STI tests, prescription services, and drop-in appointments. Some schools even offer extensive wrap-around services, such as stress management, counseling, and nutrition. A few really awesome schools offer free meditation and yoga classes for students, so inquire about what's available.

Unfortunately, community colleges rarely offer health centers, but you may still get a discount at your local doctor's office with your student ID.

If You Need Legal Services

Many universities offer free legal advice to students for matters such as landlord-tenant issues, consumer protection, alcohol use and abuse, and many other issues. Inquire with your adviser or dean to see if your school offers these services.

Sadly, few community colleges offer these services, but inquire with a trusted adviser or counselor, just in case they might know of a resource you could access.

If You Need Counseling

Most schools offer free counseling to students, and many also offer crisis centers or hotlines as well.

If You Want Recreation/Exercise

Most schools offer campus recreation centers where you can take low-cost or even free fitness and wellness classes.

Your school may also allow you free or low-cost access to exercise equipment, sport courts, and exercise classes with just a flash of your student ID.

If You Need Job Search Help

Most schools have a Career Services Support Center that provides free job-help services to students. They usually offer a wide variety of services, such as:

- Résumé-Building
- Interviewing Techniques and Mock Interviews
- Job Search Strategies
- Cover Letter Clinics
- Free printing and other computer-related services for job searches

---

Other Issues

We've covered the most frequently encountered issues you might face in college, but every person has a unique situation, so if you're facing an issue that we haven't covered, see the chart below. I also encourage you to do your own research as well to ensure you get the help you need.

Need Help With This?	Ask These People!	Find Them Here:
Understanding financial aid issues or working through problems with your financial aid	Financial aid counselor	In the Financial Aid Office
Registering for classes	1) Academic Adviser 2) Registration Online Chat or "Help" Line	1) In the "Admissions" or Student Services Center at your college 2) The number should be listed on your college's website (some colleges also offer online chatting, too!)

(*Continued*)

(*Continued*)

Need Help With This?	Ask These People!	Find Them Here:
Trouble with understanding class material	1) Your instructor 2) Tutors at the college's Tutoring Lab—often, it's free!	1) Their office hours (see the course syllabus to find out when these are, or just ask!) 2) Almost every college has a Tutoring Lab, although it might be called something else. Ask your instructor or search the college's website to find out where it is and when it's open.
Finding daycare for my kids	Your academic adviser or Office of Dean of Students	Find out if your college has a childcare center, and if so, where is it, and how you can get your children enrolled
Choosing a Major	Your academic adviser	Admissions Center
Learning disabilities	Student Accessibility Services Counselor (if you have no idea who this person is, ask your instructor, adviser, or counselor)	Your college's office of Student Accessibility Services or Student Disability Services

Suggested Exercise

1) **Check your school's website and search for "tuition emergency" or "textbook assistance."**

   Look over the information and keep it handy, in case you or someone you know ever needs it.

   If your school doesn't offer any type of emergency assistance, suggest that they do so. You can make this suggestions either via your trusted adviser/dean/professor, or, even better, write to the board of regents or other governing body directly to share your ideas.

2) **Make your own help list or chart.**

   Get out a sheet of paper and at least two pens of different colors. With the first colored pen, make a list or a chart of any questions, issues, or problems you're having now, or that you anticipate having in the future. Then, with the other colored pen, write next to the issue or question the name of at least one person whom you might ask for help (your adviser, your professor, etc.).

3) **Reach out to those people you listed on item two above and request their assistance.**

   Call, email, or visit them in office hours, and then show up to the meeting with your questions. Take a pen and paper so you can write down their suggestions.

13 Steps to Take Now to Secure a Job after Graduation

IN THIS CHAPTER, YOU WILL LEARN:

- How to build an impressive résumé
- Ways to gain interviewing practice
- Tips to land experience in your field *before* earning your degree
- Ways to ensure your online "face" is impressive
- Develop a job-search philosophy that ensures your ultimate success

With all the hard work you're putting into your schoolwork, you no doubt want to secure a great position after you graduate. The question is *how*...

The mistake many students make is they wait until they've graduated, or are just about to walk onto the stage, before they start thinking about how to land that amazing new position.

Instead, why not start thinking about—and preparing to land—that great new position right now?

We'll go over six steps to help you do just that. However, you don't necessarily need to follow the steps in this order. Complete them as you can, when you can, and slowly, you'll move yourself toward that fantastic new career.

Step One: Start Building a Great Résumé—Right Now

Don't wait until right before (or even after!) graduation to start working on your résumé. There will probably be enough pressure on you to land a job when graduation draws near, so wouldn't it be great if you already had a nice, beautifully lined résumé, ready to send out to employers?

Here's how you can begin building that beautiful résumé right now:

a) **Look at examples of successful colleagues' résumés**

Check out the résumés of others within your field. Their résumés will give you ideas of what items could appear on yours. If you don't know anyone working in your field, go online and see if you can find any posted résumés to use as a guide.

Granted, you probably can't achieve every accolade your higher-level colleagues have, but what items on their lists might you be able to work toward right now?

b) **Take résumé-building classes**

Résumé-building classes will teach you how to properly format and design your résumé, and they'll also help you get ideas on how to actually fill it in, too.

Check with your career counselor's office or search your college's website for opportunities at your school, and then check your wider community, too. Many local libraries, community groups, and workforce organizations also offer free résumé classes. You can also look for online videos or webinars that teach smart résumé building.

The more of these classes you attend, the more ideas you'll get and the more varied your résumé will be. Most classes also provide sample résumés, too, so they'll ensure you'll get plenty of materials to study, and many classes offer mock interviews in which you can practice honing your interviewing skills as well.

c) **Get another set of eyes on your résumé**

Another great way to build your résumé is simply to let others take a look at it. Your professors, career counselors, employers, friends, colleagues, fellow students, and family are all potential résumé readers. (You can also hire a professional résumé builder to help as well, though you might want to hold off on that option until you have plenty of items to list on it.)

Even if your résumé is completely empty, your readers can ask you questions and help you generate ideas about the many activities, skills, and abilities you've acquired but may not have thought to add to your résumé. They'll also give you an outsider perspective on how you're presenting yourself on paper.

Having someone else look at your résumé also helps you catch any errors. Besides, you never know if your reader might just be so impressed with your initiative and drive to succeed that they hear about an opportunity in your field and recommend you for it!

d) **Don't pad!**

"**Résumé padding**" is the act of adding completely false or grossly exaggerated information about one's accomplishments to a résumé. Since you're getting an early start on writing your résumé, you won't likely need or want to pad, which is great because padding causes many problems:

1) Padding is highly stressful, since padders worry they'll be asked about the false items.

2) Padding rarely works since most employers know all about padding and see through it.

3) Padding starts you out on the wrong foot with colleagues. When you give false information on your résumé, you're being dishonest, which isn't a great way to begin a relationship.

4) Padding is hard to take back later, and it may follow you for the rest of your career.

Step Two: Attend Professional Events

Professional events are a great way to learn more about your field, connect with colleagues, and get inspired about the work you'd like to do.

For these reasons, conventions, conferences, seminars, and even online webinars are potential gold mines for you.

Attending conferences is a fantastic way to keep abreast of the latest advances in your field, gain new ideas for your own role within that field, and meet other people doing work similar to what you would like to do. Often, you can also find out about job openings and connect directly with employers.

Even more impressive than being an attendee at these conferences and conventions is to be a *presenter*.

How?

When you attend a conference, keep that list of sessions and look over the topics. What topics might *you* present on that are similar in vein, but unique to you and your knowledge and skillset?

Make a list, and then check the conference website to see when they are accepting proposals. Then, follow their instructions and send in your proposal! If you're nervous about doing this, enlist your favorite professor's help, and also remember you have to start somewhere. If your proposal is rejected, at least you'll gain the experience of having tried, and then next time, you'll do even better. Like most things, you'll get better at presentation proposals with practice.

If you don't feel comfortable presenting by yourself, approach a fellow student or two, or even your professors. See if they would be interested in doing a joint presentation with you.

Giving your first presentation may seem scary, but it's definitely an impressive line to add to that résumé. Besides, you never know when a potential employer might be in the audience, listening to your stellar ideas. And, even if they're not, the act of putting together and conducting the presentation will develop your communication skills, increase your knowledge, and strengthen your overall confidence.

The downside of attending conferences and conventions is that they can be expensive—very expensive. However, many of them offer grants and scholarships for attendees, and you can also check with your employer or school to see if they offer stipends for attending. If you're already working within your field, chances are good your employer might just pay for the entire trip! If not, try to find local or regional conferences within your industry. They're usually more affordable and often within driving distance, and they have the added benefit of allowing you to meet people working in your field in your area.

Step Three: Gain Relevant Professional Experience

It's always a challenge to gain actual work experience in an industry when you have no experience. Most employers don't want to take a chance on a newbie, but the good news is that you can indeed gain experience before graduation.

How?

Check into internships, work-study programs, volunteering, tutoring, and other entry-level opportunities.

We'll go over each of these briefly below, but I encourage you to do your own research into them as well.

a) **Internships**

Getting great grades in school is wonderful, but often you'll find that employers care less about your grades and more about work experience. After all, nothing proves that you can indeed do the job—and do it well—better than the fact that you've *already* done it.

Although most internships do not offer a monetary paycheck, they pay dividends in many other important benefits—hands-on experience, increased knowledge, and connections within the field. They also give you an impressive item to list for that all-important résumé.

b) **Work-Study**

Many schools offer **work-study programs**, which allow students an opportunity to gain valuable work experience while pursuing a college degree.

Some colleges offer work-study jobs strictly on campus, while others offer both on and off-campus work. Some schools may match students to jobs, but many others require the student to find, apply, and interview for positions themselves. Contact your financial aid office or the student employment center to inquire about the rules and opportunities at your school.

c) **Volunteering**

Did you know that many volunteer gigs can be as little as **one hour per month?**

Did you also know volunteering is one of the best ways to gain experience in your field, increase your knowledge, and make connections?

If you can possibly spare an hour or two per month, check your local area and see what opportunities are open in your field, and try to be as precise as possible. For example, if you're hoping to become a pediatric nurse in a major hospital, see if you can find a volunteer position working with kids in a large hospital—perhaps even the very hospital where you'd like to be hired. Even if the volunteer gig doesn't lead to a job, it will undoubtedly lead to experience and contacts—both of which will almost certainly help you land a great position later.

Aside from these nice benefits, doing the actual work you want to do in the future will let you know how well you actually like it (or not!). It will also reveal your current skill level in the work and give you the opportunity to increase those skills, without fear of being fired.

Volunteering jobs also give you nice talking points for interviews when asked about your experiences in the field.

Aside from all this, volunteering is fun and highly rewarding because you'll see firsthand you're making a real difference in your community.

d) **Tutoring**

Many people think that only those who want to become teachers or professors should try tutoring, but that is not the case. Working one-on-one with others as a tutor is a great way to not only get work experience but also increase your social, communication, and critical thinking skills.

By tutoring, you'll learn to develop a rapport with a wide range of different people; you'll discover how to approach concepts from different angles, and you'll see how others understand and make sense of those concepts, too. Explaining concepts to others also builds your verbal acuity and helps you gain a deeper understanding of the material yourself.

Tutoring also develops leadership and critical thinking abilities that translate beautifully to professional environments.

Aside from these benefits, teaching others is highly rewarding and builds your confidence. It's a great way to meet other people and to potentially network, too, so, if you have the time and inclination, look into tutoring opportunities.

Step Four: Join a Club, Group, or Organization in Your Field

When you join a club or organization in your field, you gain several benefits:

a) **You'll make contacts within your field**

As a member of the club, you'll meet other students, professors, and industry professionals. These fellow members will not only be interesting to talk to about your field, but could also give you leads on jobs, serve as recommenders, or share other cool opportunities they've heard about in the industry.

b) **You'll sharpen your knowledge of your field**

The purpose of most of these types of groups or clubs is to help their members gain deeper knowledge of the field—and often these groups offer the most recent, cutting edge knowledge. Sadly, the textbooks that you read in college are often years behind the actual advances occurring out in the field. (This is especially true in medicine and science). Yet, when you spend time talking with others who actually work in the field or know people who do, you gain an insider perspective that will expand your understanding of the most current trends within your field—trends that may not be covered in class materials.

c) **It will probably point you to other, further opportunities in your field**

Many groups have their own exclusive scholarships, grants, workshops, jobs, and other opportunities that *only* members can access. When you join, you automatically have access to all of these perks.

Step Five: Build a Successful Online "Face" for Yourself

You probably already know you should be careful what you post on social media, but did you know that, according to a recent Career Builder Survey[1], almost *half* of employers use social media to research candidates?

Further, Career Builder found that many employers actually rejected candidates based on their personal social media page activity. They listed offenses such as these: maligning current or former coworkers and/or employers, inappropriate posts, or photos they deemed "provocative" or "lewd."

If you feel this is a violation of the candidate's rights to free speech and expression, I agree with you. However, until this practice is illegal, we should be mindful of our social media activity to minimize our employers' interference in our personal lives.

Here are some suggestions on how to do that:

a) **Keep your social media "faces" separate**

Have one social media account for your personal life, and another for your professional life.

Don't in any way link the two accounts (via phone numbers, emails, or other easily identifiable personal information, including your name). For your personal account, come up with a nickname that only your friends know and post under that name, rather than your professional name.

(We'll go over more tips on how to design your professional page below.)

b) **Only share sensitive information and pictures with specific friends**

You can control who sees what on your social media accounts by blocking certain people from posts or photos, so be sure you do that. Also, be especially careful with your profile picture and other components that you can't hide from the public.

If you're not sure what's private and what's public, log into your account and click on "help." The help desk can walk you through it.

c) **Edit your old updates**

If you've had potential troublesome posts that you'd like to remove, change your settings so that you limit old posts showing up anywhere on your timeline.

d) **Control "tagging" on Facebook**

Sometimes, the problem on social media is other people. They take what they think are "hilarious" photos or write questionable posts and then tag you to them, thus besmirching your reputation without your knowledge or permission. If this is the case, remove the tag, and ask the person not to do it again. Then, select the option "Review posts friends tag you in" under "Privacy." This way, the site must ask your permission before publicly tagging you.

Tips for building your professional social media page:

a) **Post only great content**

Share articles, pictures, or memes that amuse, intrigue, or inspire you. Sharing things you love and find interesting will help others to better connect with you, and you won't have to worry if your employer finds your page. In fact, you may build such a great page that you hope they do find it!

b) **Keep it G-Rated**

Avoid references to drinking, drug use, etc., and don't share or "like" comments that are (or could be interpreted as) sexist, racist, or ageist.

c) **Carefully choose photos**

You don't necessarily need to wear a suit or dress in your profile picture, but you should definitely present a neat, clean, professional appearance with an appropriate background. It's okay to have pictures of friends or family, but just be careful how many and what type these are. Pictures of you in your bikini at the beach are *not* appropriate, but snapshots from your five-year-old niece's birthday probably are.

Limit, too, the number of selfies. If every photo you share online is a selfie, others may perceive you as self-absorbed.

d) **It's a small world, after all…**

Even if your profile is set to private, remember that friends and friends of friends can and will see your posts if they are "liked" by someone with whom they are friends. You've probably heard about social media stories "going viral"? Gossip and stories spread like wildfire, so bear in mind that just because you set your profile to private and aren't "friends" with a potential employer doesn't mean they might not be able to see what you've posted or hear about it from a mutual friend.

e) **Be careful what you "like"**

Other people can indeed see our likes, so think before you "like" posts, pages, or photos. All of this data is undoubtedly being collected, and who knows how it will be used in the future...

f) **If you don't have anything nice to say...**

You know the saying. Avoid ranting or complaining on your page. Making your anger public via social media helps no one. If you need to vent, talk to a friend or get a good notebook and write it out that way—don't put it on the Internet.

g) **Get a LinkedIn page**

Most people consider LinkedIn the top professional networking site, so get yourself a profile and keep it up-to-date. Be as active as possible on the site so you can meet new people, stay in the loop, and potentially find new job opportunities.

Step Six: Complete—Don't Compete

Many job-hunting and résumé writing books and articles will ask you this question: How will you, the job seeker, distinguish yourself from your competition (aka other job seekers)?

These writers will then launch into a passionate diatribe in which they claim that your main task as a job seeker is to figure out how to "beat" out other job applicants because they're your "competition." Then, they'll direct you to shape yourself into the "best competitor" that employers will want so you can "win" the job.

This is exactly the **wrong** philosophy to adopt regarding your career search.

This strategy ignores *you*—your interests, your abilities, and your desires—and instead it puts all the power in the hands of a phantom employer. It also pits you against your fellow job seekers who, by the way, are probably soon going to be your colleagues. Instead of trying to "beat" them, you'd be much better off supporting, helping, and learning from them, but we'll come back to this point in a second.

The most serious problem with the "Become a competitor!" mindset is this one: Instead of it requiring you to ask yourself what *you* find interesting, engaging, and intriguing in your field, it demands you ask what your prospective employer wants.

After all, these competitor-minded people will tell you, the employer is the one who makes the hiring decisions.

Yet, that is not entirely true.

You, as the job seeker, also have power. You will decide whether you accept a job or not. The employer may have the money to pay you a salary, but you have something they want, too: expertise, ability, and skills. They are not the only ones with power here—you have power, too, but only if you realize it and wield it wisely.

When it comes time to interview, it's really a two-way street. The employer will interview you, but you should interview them, too. Ask:

- What kind of benefits do they offer you?
- Are there promotion opportunities?
- Will they value and tap into your particular skillsets, talents, and creativity? How?

If not, why work for them?

After all, isn't that why you're in college working so hard after all—to get a job you love and that you'll excel in doing?

Besides, if you focus exclusively on what employers want, you'll run into several problems:

a) **You'll waste a lot of time guessing**

The truth is that you can't possibly know what your prospective employer(s) will want. There are general traits most employers want—qualified, hardworking, intelligent, creative, strong communication skills, likable, etc. However, what particular skillsets they want is probably unknown. First, you probably have no idea who your prospective employer is, and since that is likely the case, how can you possibly predict what someone you've never met wants?

Second, even if you do know who this employer is, are you certain that the people making hiring decisions today will be making them in a year, two years, or three years?

Third, what people *say* they want publicly and what they *actually* want are often two completely different things.

b) **You'll waste a lot of time and energy developing skills or special expertise that you may not necessarily care about**

If some employer supposedly wants skills X, Y, and Z, and you spend two years acquiring those skills, despite the fact that you could care less about them, what will you do if the employer changes his/her mind before you get the job? This happens probably more than most of us like to think.

In fact, I see this happen frequently in higher education. The deans, executives, and vice presidents at colleges and universities attend an education conference and come back all excited over some new trend that swept through their conference. They'll then swear up and down they're going to implement this exciting new breakthrough. They form committees and design websites, talking the new project up to the skies, but, then, six months to a year later, nothing has really changed, and they've forgotten the great "new" change that so excited them initially. All the people they were supposed to hire never did get hired, or they simply were hired for a year with grant (temporary) funds, and now they're out of work.

So, instead of thinking constantly about what your employer wants, in the longer term you'll be better off thinking about what *you* want. What workshops, internships, volunteer positions, certifications, or other credentials and opportunities interest *you*? What work or experiences get you excited and would help you further your knowledge in the field?

Yes, you should consider what prospective employers want in you, but *considering* it and letting it run your life are completely different things.

For all these reasons, don't think of growing your résumé as a list of things you must do to "beat" out others to "compete" in the job market. Instead, see all the steps you're taking to building your résumé as a means to completing your training and development. Make your career building about *completing* your goals, not competing against others.

This way, you'll focus on harnessing your skills, sharpening your abilities, and growing your knowledge of your field so that you feel fulfilled and complete, not working tirelessly to beat out some phantom other person.

When you enter opportunities with *this* positive energy and are genuinely interested in growing and learning rather than "beating out" others or just adding a line to your résumé, you'll get more out of the experience. And, ironically, you'll distinguish yourself in doing this because you'll stand out. Most other people are in a zombie-like trance of attempting to simply beat out everyone else. When you're different and genuinely interesting in developing yourself and contributing to your field, you'll get noticed—and you'll probably be much happier, too.

Suggested Exercise

1) Go online and research what résumé writing classes are offered in your area over the next few months. Sign up for at least two of them and attend.
2) Research the résumés of at least two successful professionals in your industry. Study their accomplishments, awards, and experience. Make a list of ways you could replicate their accolades and begin building your own résumé.
3) Start writing your résumé. Include skills, abilities, knowledge, education, and work experience on it. Then, get someone you trust to look it over. Keep editing and making changes until you feel proud of the results.

4) Research conferences, seminars, conventions, and/or webinars in your field that you could attend in the next six months. Brainstorm ways you could pay for attending, such as applying for grants or scholarships, getting a stipend from your employer, etc. Also think about how you could handle babysitters, covered shifts, or other concerns that might stop you from attending.

5) Check out the websites for the conferences you'd like to attend and study past-year offerings. Make a list of the most interesting presentations and brainstorm ideas for presentations *you* could potentially give at the conference. Give yourself a reasonable deadline (such as six months or one year). Then, actually start to write a proposal for the conference. Get a trusted friend or colleague to look over it when it's ready, and then submit it! Enlist the help of your professors, boss, or fellow students on your project.

Note

1 Read the full article here: https://careerbuilder.com/share/aboutus/pressrelea sesdetail.aspx?ed=12%2f31%2f2013&id=pr766&sc_cmp1=cb_pr766_&sd=6 %2f26%2f2013&siteid=cbpr

Section III
Succeeding Beyond College

14 Keep Moving on Up

IN THIS CHAPTER, YOU WILL LEARN HOW TO

- Keep—and actually enjoy—that awesome job you worked so hard to get
- Earn promotions, awards, and other accolades
- Adapt, grow, and evolve so you succeed in *any* environment

Landing a wonderful new job is a great and impressive accomplishment to celebrate, but once the excitement wears off, you'll be faced with a couple of crucial questions:

How do you *keep* that awesome new job you worked so hard to get?
How do you earn promotions, win awards, and actually *enjoy* your new career?

Most career books are strangely silent on these questions. Instead, they focus on the search, search, search for that new job. They offer little, if any, advice on how to keep it and/or get promoted once you win it.

Granted, each position is unique, as is each individual, but in this chapter, we'll go over ten general steps that will help you keep that fantastic new job—*and* keep moving on up.

Be a Life-Long Learner

Many college graduates are surprised to find that instead of feeling excited after graduation, they're disappointed. They *miss* college. They don't necessarily miss the stress, the deadlines, and the worry about grades, but they miss the growth, the challenge, the progress.

The good news is that this growth is *not* dependent on being a college student. You can keep it going long after graduation, and without a hefty tuition bill to pay!

In fact, not only can you continue to grow, you must.

The job market is continually changing, as is the world around us. To keep up with those changes and adapt accordingly is crucial. In fact, that's the real secret to success, in both your professional and personal lives: Keep developing.

How can you do that?

We'll go over some suggestions below, but I encourage you to make your own list and start pursuing those things that interest and excite *you* because that's the best way to keep learning and growing—follow your interests.

- **Read books, newspapers, essays, articles, and magazines**

  Make a list of the ideas, topics, or people that interest you and research them. If you prefer online research, find a reputable blog writer, online news source, or website. If you prefer hands-on reading, locate the best local bookstores and spend time each month browsing. Get a library card and check out some books on the topic. Then, discuss these ideas with others and/or write about them in a journal or start your own blog.

- **Listen to podcasts, talks, audio books, sermons, and lectures**

  Hearing the innovations, ideas, and discoveries of others is one of the best ways to learn and feel inspired. These topics make great conversation pieces, and having discussions about ideas is one of the best ways to keep your critical thinking skills sharp.

  You'll likely find millions of sources of information, but I highly recommend TED Talks. They're among the best, most informative (and interesting) talks on the web. They're also short (18 minutes or less), and they cover topics from science to romantic love to business to social issues. (View/listen to them here: https://www.ted.com/)

- **Join groups (either online or in person)**

  Locate groups of people discussing topics that interest you. That way, you will meet new people and have opportunities to strike up conversations with experts and novices alike.

  You'll likely find millions of groups online, but you might check Meetup.com, Facebook Groups, or subject-specific chat rooms. Local groups' websites are a great source, too.

- **Take classes**

  Your company and even organizations within your community most likely offer enrichment classes to help you keep your learning ongoing. When these are offered, take advantage of them whenever you can, whether for professional or personal enrichment.

  If you're seeking classes for your professional development in particular, check with your employer. Most companies also offer on-demand webinars, videos, and other training materials, and bosses notice who takes advantage of these, and who does not.

  Online learning platforms such as Udemy and Master Class also offer a plethora of classes on virtually any topic you can name.

Stay Professionally Active

Stay relevant, marketable, and on the cutting edge by being professionally active. Here's how:

- **Attend conferences, workshops, seminars, and trainings**

   By attending, you'll pick up new knowledge and credentials, which will impress colleagues and bosses. Plus, the more you know about your field, the more empowered you are to do your job—and the more likely people will start seeing you as an expert and leader. They'll soon be asking you questions and seeking your advice, and once that happens, you're on your way to that promotion, award, and/or raise.

- **Specialize to develop precise expertise**

   Many people make the mistake of trying to be a jack-of-all-trades, learning a little bit about everything but learning a lot about nothing. Instead, discover your natural aptitude and interests—and focus there. Learn everything you can about one particular area of expertise within your field. Specialize.

   Become the go-to person for a specific topic, subject, or area.

   Not only does this specialization distinguish you, but it also helps you become more marketable to employers who might be searching for experts in that field. Even if you don't want to change jobs, it never hurts to have an offer that you can use as leverage at your current job.

- **Join groups and other professional organizations**

   Do your research and find a national, state, or regional professional group for your field, and join.

   Attend their meetings and take any trainings they offer. Often, these groups have conferences each year, and by registering you'll gain access to a huge bank of online materials and webinars.

Find a Mentor

A **mentor** is a trusted expert who gives you excellent, non-biased, professional advice to guide you in the right direction at work. This person is someone who works in your field, with probably at least a year or more of experience than you. This person should be someone you trust and admire, someone whose advice is truly valuable.

When you find this awesome person, see if they'd be willing to go to lunch, grab a coffee, or go to happy hour and let you "pick their brain" so to speak. Probably, they will be flattered and agree. If they don't, try a couple of times, and then if they're not into it, move on to someone else.

Granted, it can be hard to find this amazing person, but it's worth the time, so keep looking!

Establish Positive Relationships with Colleagues

How important are your relationships with your colleagues? If you said they are crucial, you're correct!

In fact, research from Harvard Business School suggests that likability at work is more important than most of us realize. More accurately, the research found that being liked at work is good, but avoiding being _disliked_ is crucial. The researchers put it this way: "If someone is strongly disliked, it's almost irrelevant whether or not she is competent; people won't want to work with her" (Casciaro and Lobo 1 2005).

In other words, we need to work on cultivating likability at work.

Listen to Everyone's Ideas

Few people need to be told to listen carefully to the boss's ideas. Yet, the boss is not the only person at work with great insights. The young administrative assistant who answers the phone probably knows more about what questions customers and other employees have than the boss does. The intern who just started a month ago knows firsthand whether company training is effective or not. Both of these lower-level employees are probably smarter, wiser, and more insightful than most of your colleagues think they are.

In fact, these employees may have the exact answer you're looking for, so don't overlook them once you're past entry-level. They can often help you move up—sometimes even faster than your boss.

Be a Mentor

Just as you would like someone to be a mentor to you, be a mentor to someone else. No matter where you are in your career, someone is behind you and could use your support and advice.

Seek out someone new in your organization, befriend a junior colleague, or visit your old school and offer to speak with the current students.

Not everyone has a support system, so even having just one person in their corner can make a huge difference. You could be that person. Be a sounding board, or just a cheerleader, whatever they need. Although they'll learn a great deal from you, most likely you will learn a great deal from them, too, and in the process, you're cultivating leadership experience.

Be Careful of the Company You Keep at Work

Be respectful and kind to everyone at work, but spend the majority of your time with the positive, upbeat people, rather than the faultfinders. Complainers are a dime a dozen, but people with optimistic, uplifting attitudes are rare gems. Their positive vibes will rub off on you, and you'll not only be happier but also more creative, too.

Avoid the coworkers who spend hours gossiping and complaining, and don't waste your precious time and energy doing either of these useless activities. This time and energy could be better invested in learning a new skill or just relaxing. You worked too hard to get where you are to become a nitpicker.

Develop a Professional Development (PD) Plan

Where do you want to be professionally in five years? How about ten years? Twenty?

Now, consider this question: How are you going to get there?

If you don't have a P.D. (Professional Development) plan, chances are, you won't get where you want to go. So, start creating that plan right now.

This plan will not only help you get a higher-level position, it'll help you grow and learn as a professional in your field, which will impress your bosses and make your current position more enriching, too.

Each individual is different, so you'll need to design your own plan, catered to your field and personality, but here are some ideas to get you started:

To make this P.D. plan:

- **Outline your goals**
  - What specifically do you want to accomplish?
  - What position(s) do you want to have?
  - What skills would you like to learn (or must you learn)?
  - What is your timeline?
- **Ask yourself: Why do you want to accomplish these things?**
  - Be honest!
    - Don't spend five years developing skills you don't actually care about just because you *think* they'll get you a promotion
- **Outline the steps to gaining those goals**
  - Do you need certain certifications, classes, or trainings?
  - If there's certain software you must master, how can you learn it?
  - Classes?
  - Webinars or conferences? (Perhaps the company will pay?)
  - Would a colleague currently using it teach you?
- **Implement your plan**
  - Register for those classes, trainings, or workshops
  - Put those skills into action at work and/or home
    - The more you practice those new skills, the more adept you'll become
- **Be vocal about your new knowledge—and share it!**
  - Share with your boss and colleagues all that you're learning and why it's important to you

- Offer to conduct trainings and workshops to share your knowledge with others
    - Becoming a trainer highlights you as a leader and trusted expert, which helps pave the way to promotions
- **Update your résumé with new skills**
    - Add those new credentials, certifications, or trainings to your résumé
        - If you need to change jobs, prospective employers will be impressed that you're so professionally active
        - This additional training and expertise also strengthens your argument that you deserve a nice raise

Keep in Touch with Supporters

Remember all those awesome people who helped you along the way—professors, advisers, counselors, classmates, tutors, etc.? Don't forget about them now that you're a bigwig! Reach out to them often. Let them know how you're doing.

Did you pass an important certification exam? Land a fantastic new job? Score a big raise? Share news of these accolades with your supporters. Send out a mass email letting everyone know—and be sure to thank them for their role. Let them know you haven't forgotten they helped you get where you are.

Sadly, few people do this, but those who do really stand out.

Aside from being a nice thing to do, keeping in touch to say "thank you" and update your supporters is actually quite a wise career move, too. By keeping your supporters in the loop about your progress, you're increasing their investment in you. These supporters will thus be much more likely to re-invest in you in the future. That's not necessarily the goal here, but wouldn't it be good to know you have that support, if you ever need it?

Develop a Happiness Habit

Did you know that research shows that being happier actually leads to greater productivity and success at work?

And, the reverse is also true: Lower happiness means lower productivity (Sgroi 1).

We've focused so far on developing professionally, but don't forget, too, that it's important to actually enjoy living your life. After all, you went back to school not just to get a better job but to have a better life, yes?

So, don't always be working, working, working, telling yourself you must work because you want your family to have a "better life some day." That better life starts now—and it must include you.

Show up for the important family events, and be there for your loved ones. Don't make working or earning money the be-all, end-all of your existence.

Spend time with the people you love and value, and take time to laugh and have fun. Go out to eat. Take in a show. Enjoy a bottle of wine. Eat a slow dinner. Sit by the fire. Take time to slow down and enjoy the fruits of your labor. Not only will you be a better worker, you'll be a happier person overall.

Working hard is fine, but you should also enjoy the benefits of that hard work, too. Otherwise, why did you go back to school to begin with? You can get more money, but you can't get back time, so use it wisely.

Suggested Exercise

1) **Make a list of your interests—personal and professional.**
   Dig deep, and list everything that interests you, even if you have no idea how to pursue that interest yet (or if you even want to pursue it!). For example, here's one student's list:

   Pediatric nursing
   Medicine
   Cuban cooking
   Playing the violin
   U.S. politics
   Ancient Aztec history
   Children's literature
   Tai Chi
   Eastern music
   Swing dancing
   Interior decorating
   Cake baking
   Woodworking
   General self-improvement

2) **Pick your top three interests and then research some possible sources of information.**
   Try TED talks, webinars, magazines, YouTube videos, books, blogs, vlogs, etc.
3) **Carve out some time (perhaps half an hour) each week to spend on developing these hobbies.** Enlist the help of friends or family and/or get them involved. Is there a free workshop in your area on one of your hobbies? Why not bring the kids, spouse, or a friend with you?
4) **Write out a detailed P.D. plan of where you'd like to be in five years.**
   To the best of your ability, list the steps it will take to get there. If you're not sure, start doing some research and fill in these steps the best you can. Keep an eye out for a possible mentor whom you could ask for help in making your plan, or if you have someone in mind already, contact him/her and ask for assistance in developing your P.D. plan.

Section IV
Additional College Resources

Appendix A
College Vocabulary Glossary

FINANCIAL AID

Financial aid	Money available to help pay for college, usually from the U.S. government, but can also be from your college's own funds, too. You can use financial aid to pay for anything associated with your classes: books, tuition, fees, supplies, etc.
Financial aid package	Total amount of financial aid you receive to help pay for college costs; it includes grants, loans, and/or scholarships that you received
F.A.F.S.A.	Free Application for Federal Student Aid is used to determine financial aid from federal resources and from many state resources. Many colleges also require it for institutional aid
Grants	A form of financial aid that does not have to be repaid, as long as you complete your classes—and pass
Loans	A form of financial aid that must be repaid *with interest*
Scholarships	A form of financial aid that does not have to be repaid, and is generally based on academic skills, but you can also often find scholarships for your athletic abilities, background, age, gender, nationality, spiritual beliefs, or race
Full-time student	Students taking 12 or more credit hours per semester
Part-time student	Students taking fewer than 12 credit hours per semester

---

ACADEMIC

College placement or assessment test	Determines how prepared you are for college-level work. Most community colleges require students to take a placement test before enrolling
Credit hours	Each course has a certain number of credit hours attached to it. (Most college classes are three credit hours.) You can often tell how many credit hours will be earned by looking at the course number. (Often, the first number is the number of credit hours.)

(Continued)

(Continued)

ACADEMIC

	For example, English 301 will earn you 3 credit hours; Spanish 501 will earn you 5 credits; Biology 401 will earn you 4 credits.
	If you took all three of these classes together in one semester, you'd be taking 12 hours total $(3+5+4=12)$
	When you pass the class, you earn those credits, which will count toward earning your certificate or degree
Major	The primary subject you choose to study in college, such as nursing, engineering, psychology, or computer science, etc.
	A majority (but not all) of your college courses will be related to your major
Associate's degree	Usually takes two years to complete, by earning around 60 credit hours (but the number of credits depends on the major, and sometimes the institution)
	There are three types of Associate's degrees:

Associate in Science (A.S.)
Popular majors within this degree include:

- Nursing
- Accounting
- Criminal Justice
- Business Administration

Associate in Applied Science (A.A.S.)
Popular majors within this degree include:

- Paralegal
- Dental Hygiene
- Web Design
- Veterinary Technology

Associate in Arts (A.A.)
Popular majors within this degree include:
- Psychology
- Graphic Design
- General Studies

Bachelor's degree	Usually takes about four years to complete, by earning around 120 credit hours. You cannot typically get a Bachelor's degree at a two-year community college; however, you can usually use your credits from the community college towards a Bachelor's degree. In other words:

two years at community college

+

another two years at university

=

four Years (Bachelor's degree)

(Continued)

(*Continued*)

ACADEMIC

The three most popular types of Bachelor's degrees are:

Bachelor of Science (B.S. degree)
Popular majors within this degree include:

- Computer Science
- Nursing
- Chemical Engineering
- Business

Bachelor of Arts (B.A. degree)
Popular majors within this degree include:

- English
- Psychology
- Communications

Bachelor of Fine Arts (B.F.A. degree)
Popular majors within this degree include:

- Graphic Design
- Animation
- Game Design

Certificate — A document granted by an institution proving the recipient earned a certain number of approved credits. It usually takes approximately one year to earn a certificate, though completion times vary by school, student, and discipline.

Coursework is typically focused on the area of study. No generalized coursework (such as math, history, or government) is typically required.

Popular Certificates:

- Accounting Clerk
- Office Clerk
- Welder
- HVAC
- CAD (Computer Aided Design)
- Automotive Technician
- EMT

Certificates can be a great way to boost your income —and confidence—by earning a quick college credential. However, don't assume that just because a college offers a certain certificate that it's valuable. This is sadly not necessarily true. (It *should* be true, but unfortunately, it's not.)

Some certificates are highly valuable, and others are not—and often this value depends on where you live. What's valuable to employers in my city of Austin, TX, may not be to employers in yours.

Do your research and make sure the certificate you want will actually help you get the career and/or raise and promotions you seek.

(*Continued*)

(*Continued*)

ACADEMIC

Pre-requisite class	A class required before a student may enroll in a higher-level class. For example, College Writing 1 is usually a pre-requisite for College Writing 2, or Nursing 3 would be a pre-requisite for Nursing 4
Co-requisite classes	Two or more classes that must be taken together, such as a biology lecture and lab
Online courses	Classes that meet entirely online, rather than in-person. Students log into an online platform (such as Blackboard or Google Classroom) to complete all course material, take notes, interact with their instructor and classmates, and turn in assignments.
Syllabus	A written overview of the course, including its rules, procedures, and grading; it may also include an outline of topics to be covered by the instructor and assignments to be completed by the students during the course. Think of it as the rulebook of the course.
Add/Drop Period	The time in the semester when students may add a class to their schedule or drop a class from it. Usually, this is the first week or so of the semester. During this time, if you need to change your schedule, you can. After this time is over, you usually can only drop a class, but you cannot add one. Dropping a class can have consequences, both for your G.P.A. and for your financial aid, so be sure to check your school's rules before dropping!
Your "Social"	Your social security number If you don't have one, schools can offer you an alternative ID number
"Residency Requirements"	State colleges and universities are funded with public tax dollars, so students who are residents receive reduced tuition rates. Non-residents can still attend, but they pay higher rates (sometimes double or even triple). If you're not sure if you're a resident, check the school's website and/or call the registration help line.

(*Continued*)

(*Continued*)

ACADEMIC

G.P.A. **(GRADE POINT AVERAGE)**	**G.P.A.** = <u>G</u>rade <u>P</u>oint <u>A</u>verage Every semester, you'll receive a **G.P.A.** based on the final grade you earned in each of your classes. For example, if you took two classes, then those two grades will be averaged. This average is your G.P.A. Each letter grade of "A" or "B" or "C" that you earn in your class is translated into a number scale. The higher the grade you earned, the more "points" you get. Here's how it works: • "A" = 4 points (4.0) • "B" = 3 points (3.0) • "C" = 2 points (2.0) • "D" = 1 point (1.0) • "F" = 0 points (0.0) So, if you earn an "A" and a "B" next semester in your two classes, you would receive four points for your "A" and three points for your "B." The college would then average those two scores together to figure out your G.P.A.: $(4 + 3 = 7; 7/2 = 3.5)$, so your G.P.A. would be **3.5**
"College Ready"	The student is academically prepared for college-level classes. Usually, this term refers to passing the state's college entrance exam and proving that the student has college-level skills in reading, writing, and math. If a student is not proven "college ready" in these subjects, then he/she typically must take zero-level or "developmental" classes to get him/her ready for college-level classes
Developmental or Zero-Level Classes	Classes just below college level that build students' basic skills in reading, writing, and math to prepare students for college-level work. These classes do NOT earn credits at most schools, but the grade earned may count toward a student's G.P.A.
Elective Courses	Courses a student takes by *choice*, rather than being specifically required by a degree. Different degree plans have different definitions of approved "electives," so choose electives carefully.

(*Continued*)

(*Continued*)

ACADEMIC

Auditing a course	A course taken simply for the knowledge it offers or for personal enrichment. No grade or official credit is received. Different schools have different auditing policies, so check with your institution
Final exam	The final test in a course, held at the end of the class, usually on the final course day, though timing depends on instructor and discipline. Percentage of course grade, too, is dependent on institutions and instructors, but typically final exams comprise no more than one third of students' overall final course grade
Finals Week **Or "Dead Week"**	The last week of classes each semester. Regular class meetings are typically suspended, as students are studying for and taking final exams
Freshman or first-year student	Student who has earned between 0 and 29 credit hours
Sophomore student	Student who has earned between 30 and 59 credit hours
Junior student	Student who has earned between 60 and 89 credit hours
Senior student	Student who has earned 90 or more credit hours
Transcript	The student's official record of courses taken, grades earned, and certificates or degrees awarded. Can be **official** (only when sent directly from the institution, on special paper, and bearing the school's official seal) or **unofficial** (if printed without the seal and/or on plain paper)
Undergraduate	A student who has not yet earned a Bachelor's degree. This term can also apply to the coursework and programs in which students enroll to earn a Bachelor's degree

Appendix B
Scholarships for Adult Students: Apply Now!

Below you will find a list of potential scholarships for which you can/should apply. At the end of this Appendix, you'll find some suggestions for other places you can look for scholarships as well as a reminder of the Dos and Don'ts of applying for scholarships.

Association for Non-Traditional Students in <u>Higher Education</u> (A.N.T.S.H.E.) Scholarships

Deadline: Varies
Award Amount: Varies

Requirements:
- Must be a non-traditional (adult) student

Visit:
https://myantshe.org/ANTSHE-Scholarships

Adult Skills Education Grant

Deadline: Varies
Available to: College Freshmen through College Seniors
Award Amount: $1,000

Requirements:
- At least 19 years of age
- U.S. citizen
- Have a high school diploma, a G.E.D., or pass an Ability to Benefit test and be enrolling in a participating college

Visit:
https://www.imagine-america.org/faqadult-skills-education-program/

Dr. Blanca Moore-Velez Woman of Substance Scholarship

Deadline: Varies
Available to: College Freshmen through College Seniors
Award Amount: Varies

Requirements:
- Must be female and African-American
- Must be at least 35 years of age
- Must have a minimum 3.0 G.P.A. to be eligible for this award
- Must submit a 500-word essay on the following topic: "Challenges to the Mature Student and How I Overcame Them"

Visit:
https://fastweb.com/college-scholarships/scholarships/149460

Jeannette Rankin Foundation Scholarship

Deadline: Varies
Award Amount: Varies

Requirements:
- Must be female
- Must be aged 35 or older
- Must be a low-income student pursuing a technical/vocational education, Associate's degree or first Bachelor's degree
- Must be attending a regionally or ACICS accredited school

Visit:
https://rankinfoundation.org/

P.E.O. Program for Continuing Education

Deadline: Varies
Application Year: College Junior through Graduate Students, Year 3
Award Amount: $2,000

Requirements:
- Must be female
- Must be at least 21 years of age
- Must be attending a college or university in the U.S. or Canada
- Must be a citizen of the U.S. or Canada
- Must be within 24 months of completing your educational goal

Visit:
https://www.peointernational.org/about-peo-program-continuing-education-pce

Women On Par Scholarship

Deadline: April 15
Award Amount: $1,000

Requirements:
- Must be female
- Must be aged 30 or older
- Must be attending a college or university for the first time OR returning to school after an absence to complete their technical/vocational, Associate's or Bachelor's degree

Visit:
https://lpgaamateurs.com/memberships/scholarship/

Return2College Scholarship

Deadline: September 30
Award Amount: $1,500

Requirements:
- Must enroll in college within the next 12 months
- Students may be part-time or full-time students pursuing an undergraduate or graduate degree

Visit:
http://www.return2college.com/awardprogram.cfm

General Scholarship for Higher Learning

Deadline: October 15
Award Amount: $1,500

Requirements:
- Must complete four short essays
- Must be at least 18 years old

Visit:
https://interior-deluxe.com/scholarship

AARP Foundation Women's Scholarship

Deadline: March 30

Award Amount: Varies based on eligibility factors.

Award can range from $500 to $5,000 per year. The exact amount depends on both the applicant's demonstrated financial need and the cost of the degree or training program she is enrolled in

Requirements:
- Must be low-income female, meaning personal assets and income must equal no more than 150% of the Federal Poverty Guidelines, which are available on the scholarship website
- Must be aged 50 or older by the date of their application
- Must pursue a technical, Associate's or Bachelor's degree within six months of the award date
- Applicants must complete an extremely detailed application and questionnaire that inventories educational and work background
- Applicants will answer several detailed essay questions about hardships and difficulties they have faced

Visit:
https://aarp.org/aarp-foundation/our-work/income/womens-scholarship-program/

Unigo Scholarships

Deadline: Last day of every month
Award Amount: Some $2,000 awards, some $5,000 awards

Requirements:
- Must be 21 years of age or older
- Each month, they offer a fun, creative writing contest for U.S. students. Topics include surviving a zombie apocalypse ($2,000), explaining why a college education matters ($5,000), and listing ten reasons why students should receive a scholarship ($1,500).

Visit:
https://unigo.com/scholarships/our-scholarships/?sid=sm-blog

Additional Scholarship Sources:

Check these potential sources in your life as well:
- Your school
- Your kids' school
- Your parents' school
- Your spouse's school
- Your employer
- Your spouse's employer
- Your church or religious/spiritual group
- Your groups (AARP, NAACP, Boy Scouts, Girl Scouts, Toast Master's, American Legion)

"Dos and Don'ts" of Applying for Scholarships:

Do:

- **Follow instructions to a "T"**
  - Submit on time
  - Include all required materials (essays, recommendation letters, etc.)
- **Beware scholarship scams**
  - Look for a phone number you can call for information
  - Look for proof of past winners of the scholarship; unless it's a new scholarship, there should be some indication of past winners
  - Trust your instincts; if something seems off, it probably is!
- **If legit, apply!**
  - Even if you think you won't get the scholarship, apply anyway!
    - If you don't apply, then there is a 100% chance you won't get it, but if you do apply, you just might!
    - Many scholarship funds sit unused simply because no one applied!

Don't:

- **Give out sensitive financial information**
  - **Never** give a scholarship committee your credit card, bank account number, or social security number. They have no business with this information. If you win, they can send you money via check or to your school account. If they need an identifying number, they can use your school ID number
- **Pay**
  - Legitimate scholarships don't charge fees, so don't pay **any** fee to apply

- **Accept a scholarship you never applied for**
  - Scholarships require applications and essays and recommendations. You have to *work* to get them. If someone wants to just "give" you one, something's wrong
  - If they claim your instructor recommended you, ask for the instructor's name and reach out to him/her to verify

---

IF YOU SUSPECT A SCHOLARSHIP SCAM, PLEASE HELP OTHER STUDENTS AND REPORT IT

Online:
https://ftccomplaintassistant.gov/GettingStarted?NextQID=409
&Url=%23%26panel1-2&SubCategoryID=2#crnt

By mail:
National Fraud Information Center
PO Box 65868
Washington, DC 20035

By phone:
1-800-876-7060.

For even more adult college student scholarship opportunities, visit these sites:

- https://accreditedschoolsonline.org/resources/scholarships-for-nontraditional-students/
- https://scholarships.com/financial-aid/college-scholarships/scholarship-directory/school-year/not-currently-enrolled-non-traditional-student
- http://collegescholarships.com/
- https://bigfuture.collegeboard.org/scholarship-search
- http://fastweb.com/college-scholarships/articles/non-traditional-adult-and-returning-student-scholarships
- https://careeronestop.org/toolkit/training/find-scholarships.aspx

Appendix C
Beware the Bureaucracy of Higher Education!

Adult students are the new majority on most college campuses these days. That's the good news for you, the adult student. The bad news is that few colleges and universities have adjusted to your needs.

Most of them are stuck in the past—decades and decades in the past.

They have antiquated rules and policies designed for the 18-year-old full-time student who has plenty of time on campus to jump through the 30 million hurdles set in their way to getting a college degree.

This system is the **college bureaucracy**. It's embedded within most American colleges and universities, and it often forces students to jump through hoops, navigate red tape, and complete tons of work to meet administrative policies. These policies were likely originally designed with student success in mind, but, over the years, the processes to complete them have become convoluted, complicated, and confusing.

For example, sometimes students have to travel from office to office simply to get the correct piece of paper to give to an employee at yet another office to sign. The student then must carry that signed paper across campus to return to yet *another* office and employee.

Hopefully, you will not encounter any problems with your college's bureaucracy.

However, in case you do, just know that, for now, part of going to college means dealing with red tape and navigating a confusing system that may seem, at times, to be against you.

The key is this: **Keep at it, don't give up, and don't take "no" for an answer.**

Often, if you keep trying, your sheer persistence will solve the problem.

And, keep in mind, too, that when one employee isn't helpful, that's not the end of the road. Try another, and another, and another. Simply because one employee says something is The Law of the College doesn't necessarily mean it is. Keep asking, and don't give up until your problem is resolved.

Let's go over some of the bureaucratic roadblocks you might encounter in college and ways you can potentially overcome them.

1   **Non-Transferrable Coursework or Work Experience**
   - Many adult students have taken dozens of college credits at other institutions and face an uphill battle trying to get their current school to accept those credits
   - Many other students have acquired years of work within their field and don't need the lower-level courses that cover material they mastered decades ago, but, still, the college forces them to take (and pay for) these courses, anyway

   Possible solutions:
   - Some schools are beginning to offer limited credit hours for prior learning and/or work experience
     - Check with your school to see what they offer
     - If they seem unwilling to work with you, try moving up the ladder and suggesting the policy change. Often, the people with the power to change policies are simply unaware of the problems students encounter simply because they never hear from students! Let your voice be heard
   - Veteran students, in particular, should check into what options are available for getting credit for prior knowledge and work experience

2   **Trouble with Changing Majors**
   - Some colleges require returning students to stick with their old major, even if they're no longer interested in that major

   Possible solutions:
   - If your school requires many hurdles to change your major, speak with an adviser or dean about changing these policies for adult students. Explain why the policy is problematic and have some suggested solutions in mind (changing via online services, email, etc.)
   - Don't accept this answer, either: "Because that's how it's always been." First, that's a lame and ridiculous reason, and second, the typical college student has changed, and colleges must adjust to serve the needs of their current student population

3   **Conflicting Advice**
   - Students often meet with more than one college employee (perhaps an adviser, instructor, and counselor), and each person with whom they meet may give them different advice

   Possible solutions:
   - **Be proactive**
     - Learn as much as you can about your degree requirements and your college's rules

- For example, if one adviser tells you it's a great idea to take College Algebra but another tells you that you absolutely must take Elementary Statistics, look up your degree requirements yourself and verify
  - If you're attending a community college now but plan to transfer to a university, check with that institution, too. Do they care which math class you take? (Hint: Yes, they almost certainly do!)
  - If you're still not sure, check with your department chair to verify
- **Ask follow-up questions**
  - For that adviser who likes your idea to take College Algebra, ask her *why* she thinks so. Perhaps she knows it's not a degree requirement, but she has some other reasoning for suggesting you take it. Once you understand her reasoning, you can make your decision
- **Do what *you* believe is best**
  - Your education is just that—yours. So, if you have a deep sense that there is a course you need to take but a college employee advises against it, follow your own inner wisdom. There's no telling what benefit you might gain from that course
    - A famous example is this: Steve Jobs (founder and creator of Apple Computers) felt drawn to a Calligraphy class in college. His advisers balked, telling him it was a "useless" class. He took it, anyway. Years later, he used what he learned in that "useless" class on his computer's design. He created the beautiful fonts and typography most of us take for granted on computers today! (And, some people argue this typeface feature was *the* distinguishing factor that led to Apple's early success)

4 Limited Campus Service Hours

- Many adult students attend classes at night or on the weekends, but student services, registration, financial aid, advising, and other critical college services often aren't open at these times. How, then, can adult students conduct college business?

Possible solutions:
- Check into online, 24-hour help services or after-hour "Help Desk" services
  - Many colleges offer these services but may not advertise them well
- Ask for permission at work to conduct your college business during business hours, or go during your lunch hour

- Some students have even taken the day off to handle their college business, but not all students have this luxury
- Advocate
  - If no after-hour services are offered at your school, ask why not and suggest they be added immediately
  - If needed, speak to other adult students and have them send emails and make phone calls, too

The bottom line here is this: Colleges must learn to accommodate their students, not the other way around—but that's *not* going to happen unless students demand it.

5   **"Holds" on Your Student Account**
- Holds or "blocks" on your account can prevent you from registering or even graduating. Typically, they fall into one of three categories: financial, academic, and administrative. These holds may include:
  - Library fines
  - Parking tickets
  - Missing required documentation (proof of address, high school transcript, etc.)
  - Transcript fee
  - Graduation fee

Possible solutions:

Obviously, if you can acquire what is needed (the document or money or whatever), then do that, but most likely you can't do so. Otherwise, you wouldn't have the hold! So, try these methods as well:

- **Solicit help from an insider**
  - Find a friendly adviser, coordinator, dean, or counselor and explain your situation to them. Even if they personally can't help you, they might know someone who knows someone who can
  - I've seen this time and time again—when students try to navigate the system alone, they get nowhere. But, as soon as they have an insider helping them, suddenly, the wheels are in motion. It's not necessarily fair, but it's true.
- **Do your best to follow all other rules and submit everything <u>else needed</u>**
  - Make yourself look as responsible and rule-abiding on paper as possible
    - Often, if there's simply one little problem in your way, the college is more willing to help you remove it. When there are many, though, that can be harder to overcome

- **Stay friendly and professional**
  - I know it's easier said than done, but do your best to be friendly through the mess
    - A friendly, professional student is the one who will likely get help. An angry one is easier to dismiss as combative
    - Granted, you may have the right to be angry here, but that anger probably isn't going to serve your cause
- **Go to the source**
  - For example, if it's a financial aid hold, go to financial aid and speak to them in person if at all possible (it's much harder to say "no" to someone standing in front of you!). Explain your situation and see if they will help
  - If that doesn't work, make your way up the administrative chain
    - Go to the chair of your department, the person in charge of financial aid, or the dean of students, etc. Take your case to the college president, the board of trustees, or whomever you need to get it resolved

6 **Classes Offered Only in Off Semesters**
- At some colleges or universities, not all courses students need are available every semester
  - For example, if Anna took Nursing 101 last spring, then Nursing 102 last fall, by this spring, she's ready to take Nursing 103. Yet, at her school, this class is only offered in the fall. Anna then either has to take a break this spring or take classes she doesn't need

Possible solutions:
- **Plan, Plan, Plan!**
  - Plan your schedule for each semester well in advance
  - Make sure the classes you need will be available when you need them. Don't assume all classes are available every semester— they're not!
- **Don't give up**
  - Waiting an entire semester for a course is frustrating, but in the long run, it is only one semester. Don't throw away your future over this wait
- **Take alternative courses wisely**
  - If you do get into a situation in which a class you need is not available, simply take another one that you're interested in and could benefit from the most—even if it's not on your degree plan. Granted, you may not get credit for it, but you'll acquire the knowledge and skills it offers, and who knows how those might help you in the future

7 Confusing Online Registration Systems
- Many online registration processes are confusing and difficult to navigate. Whether it's the system itself or simply remembering your username and password, these systems can pose big problems
- Calling for help isn't always possible, if students are attempting to register after working hours or on weekends

Possible solutions:
- **Instructional videos**
  - Check your college's website or YouTube for instructional videos that walk you through the registration process
  - If your college does not offer a video, suggest they do
- **Keep a password book or list**
  - Many students keep a list in their phone or email of their student ID number, username, email address, and passwords
    - Use *hints* of the passwords, if possible
      - Having your passwords and login information sitting in your phone for any hacker to easily find is not a good idea. Instead, use hints, so you know the password, but others don't. Also, get virus protection software on your phone, just in case
- **Online help chat**
  - Many schools offer online help chat 24/7. If your school does not, suggest they do
- **Make an appointment to register with an adviser**
  - If your adviser cannot meet with you at a time that works for you, politely request that they do so. If they refuse, perhaps it's time for a new adviser

Just one last thing here: Remember that most of these policies were designed with good intentions. Few college administrators want to create problems for a student. They're likely just unaware how the policies actually affect real students.

This is why it's critical you make your voice heard—for yourself and all other adult learners. If you don't, then how will college leaders know what and how to change?

Appendix D
How to Transfer to a Four-Year University

If you're attending a community college and thinking about transferring to a university, don't think for a second that you can't do it! You absolutely can!

In fact, I've known hundreds of students who have done just that, and you can, too.

Let's begin with some facts about transferring, and then we'll go over the steps to begin taking to initiate that transfer!

What is a Transfer?

A "transfer" to a university essentially means taking the two years of coursework you earned at the two-year college and transferring those credits to a university. So, for example, if you already passed your English Composition I course at your local college, you won't have to take it again at the university—as long as the university accepts the transferred credit.

Each university has its own policies for what credits they will accept as a "transfer." You can find out this information by looking at their transfer equivalency guide (more on this below).

Here are a few more transfer facts:

- Many universities have both a minimum and a maximum number of credits you can transfer
  - For example, they may not allow you to transfer until you've earned at least 30 credits, but they may not accept more than 70 credits
- This means if you already earned 60 credits at your two-year college, and the university accepts you and your 60 credits, you'll start at the university as a junior!
- When you graduate from the four-year university, *only* the university's name will appear on your degree
- Many universities will consider your G.P.A. when admitting you, but once accepted, your university G.P.A. will likely only be calculated on your *university* classes

You'll definitely want to do more research and engage the help of advisers (both at your college and the prospective university) when transferring, but let's go over some basics now on how you can begin this journey.

Ask Questions
Every answer starts with questions, so here are some questions you'll want to begin asking:

a) **What universities interest you? Why?**

Make a list of the universities that you're most interested in attending. Why do they interest you? Is it:
- The beautiful campus?
- The name fame of the school?
- The nearness to your current home?
- The small class sizes?
- The great student services?
- The reputation of your particular department within the university?

In other words, what it is you really want out of your university? Is it simply a degree with prestige? Or, do you also want to develop contacts in your field? Do you want to receive one-on-one advice from your professors, advisers, and counselors?

b) **How much does each university cost?**

Really dig in here. Find out what the **total price** will be per class, per semester (tuition, fees, books, etc.).

This is critical because some universities, even right near each other, can vary drastically in price. For example, in my city of Austin, TX, The University of Texas (a state school) is about one third the cost of St. Edward's University (a private school), only about five miles away.

c) **Is the school worth the cost?**

Many prestigious schools are also quite costly, yet the huge tuition bill may not be worth the prestige. So, if you're thinking about a high-dollar university, be sure you weigh the pros and cons of forking out that much money for that degree. It might be worth the cost, but then again, it might not be. Is there a school similarly ranked, meaning it's of equal educational quality, but perhaps not as well known (and thus more affordable)?

d) **Are certain universities prized within your field?**

In certain fields, there are particular schools considered the cream of the crop. So, graduates from these coveted institutions are practically guaranteed a job in the field. (Think Harvard Business School for business majors or MIT for computer science and/or engineering). Yet, for many fields, so long as you have the degree and the skills, the university doesn't necessarily matter. Be sure to do your homework here and find out if there is a certain school near you that would make a significant difference in helping you land that awesome new position.

e)   **What kind of accreditation does the school have?**
    Not all universities are equal, and accreditation (or lack thereof!) is a crucial factor when choosing a university. Many fly-by-night universities pop up, promising students the skies, and then a year or two later, these "universities" disappear, leaving their students with a hefty bill but no recognized, transferrable credits. Don't let this happen to you!

ALWAYS CHECK THE ACCREDITATION OF <u>ANY</u> SCHOOL YOU CONSIDER ATTENDING!

What is accreditation?
Accreditation is proof that a school has met the standards set by an accrediting agency. Essentially, accreditation tells you if the school is legitimate or not.
Almost all schools claim to have the proper accreditation to try and fool students into thinking they're legitimate, but don't let them trick you!
Here's what to look for in terms of accreditation: **Regional accreditation is better than national.**

To see if your school is regionally accredited,
    check via either of these websites:
• https://www.chea.org/search-institutions
• https://www.ed.gov/accreditation

---

f)   **What do you need to transfer?**
    Use the university's transfer website to find answers to these questions:
• When is the application deadline?
• Will the credits you earned at your two-year college be fully accepted?
• What G.P.A. do you need to get in?
• Are there any assessments you must take? If so, by when?
• What other requirements does the university have for admissions (application fees, essays, recommendation letters, etc.)?

Plan, Plan, Plan!

Now that you have an idea of what schools you'd like to attend, you're ready to begin planning that transfer. You'll need to start with a couple of items:

- Transfer guide
  - Find out what classes from your school will transfer to the university (most colleges offer online "transfer equivalency guides" via their websites)
  - What G.P.A. must you have to transfer?
  - Does the university accept transfers every semester, or only in the fall?
- Advising
  - Schedule a meeting with your current adviser as well as an adviser at your prospective new school. Go over any questions you have and ensure you're fully prepared for the transfer
- **Get admissions packet together**
  - Make a plan for getting all needed materials to the university for your admissions packet **on time!**
- **Check your new school's website** to ensure you know the proper deadlines

    Give yourself plenty of time (at least three to six months) to prepare your packet. Tracking down recommendations, taking tests, and writing essays takes time. You want to do it right, not do it rushed!
- Your packet will likely include:
  - **Admission application**
  - **Entrance exam scores**
  - **Transcript from current college**
  - **Personal essay(s)**
  - **Recommendation letter(s)**
  - **Declaration of major**
- Campus visit
  - Check out the campus overall, including classroom buildings, labs, admissions, student centers, etc.
  - See if you can get an appointment with someone in your new department (an adviser, counselor, etc.) so you can ask major-specific questions
  - Seek out current students and/or graduates to ask about job prospects

Implement!
- **Complete that admissions packet**
  - Request and submit your transcripts
  - Find recommendation letter writers
  - Begin composing those entrance essays
    - Get your favorite English instructor to look over them and help you
- **Keep up your current schoolwork**
  - Don't forget you'll be transferring your current classes, too, so keep up that great G.P.A.!
  - Current professors would make great recommenders, so don't slack off in class!

Appendix E
College Knowledge Quiz!

Instructions: Test your knowledge to see how much you learned from this book. You'll find the answer key immediately following.

Section I: Getting Started in College

1) Why do many colleges require students to take an assessment before registering for classes?

2) What is the difference between a full-time and a part-time student?

3) What is a G.P.A. and how is it calculated?

4) If Maria took two classes last semester and earned an "A" and a "B," what is her G.P.A. for that semester?

5) What's a "residency requirement"? How does it affect how much tuition you have to pay?

6) What's the difference between a certificate and a degree?

Section II: Financial Aid

1) Explain the differences between grants, loans, and scholarships.

2) How do students apply for financial aid?

3) TRUE or FALSE: Financial aid is an easy, punishment-free way to scam free money from the government. To do this, just pretend to enroll in college; then, once you get the money, drop your classes, and keep your free money! The government will never catch you, and there won't be any repercussions later.

4) TRUE or FALSE:
   If you apply for financial aid, get approved, and then don't take the money, you'll get in trouble with the government.

Section III: Your Classes

1) What is a "course schedule"?

2) Where can students find their college's course schedule?

3) Explain what a "credit hour" is.

4) About how many hours per week would you need to take a three-hour college credit course? Be sure to include in your answer time for class, homework, and studying.

5) Explain the difference between a "developmental course" and a "credit course."

6) TRUE or FALSE:

Most professors prefer their students to be young and fresh out of high school.

7) In Chapter 10 of this book, we discussed the three-part process of preparing for tests. What were those three parts? List some of the steps involved in each part to illustrate your answer.

8) TRUE or FALSE:

A syllabus is like your rule book for your classes; it spells out what the rules are and what is expected of you as a student. It also usually outlines how to get an "A" or "B" in the course.

9) Name some ways to save money on textbooks.

10) List some of the ways we discussed to manage your time successfully.

11) Brainstorm some ways that you might try to get family and friends to support your decision to go back to school.

ANSWER KEY FOR COLLEGE KNOWLEDGE QUIZ

Section I: Getting Started in College

1) **Why do many colleges require students to take an assessment before registering for classes?**

   Colleges require an assessment for placement purposes: They want to determine the students' current skill levels in the key areas of reading, writing, and math.

   If a student earns a "college ready" score on this assessment, then she is likely placed into college credit classes. If the student does not yet earn the "college ready" score, then she may be placed into developmental classes.

   It is possible for students to be placed into developmental classes in one subject (for example, in math) but then be placed in college credit classes in another subject (for example in reading and writing).

   Students can always re-take this assessment if they feel like it did not accurately measure their current skill level. This assessment is **not** an intelligence test.

2) **What is the difference between a full-time and a part-time student?**

   Full-Time = 12 credit hours or more per semester

   Part-Time = Fewer than 12 credit hours per semester

3) **What is a G.P.A. and how is it calculated?**

   G.P.A. = Grade Point Average

   Each final course grade earns the student "points' toward his/her G.P.A.:

   "A" = 4 points
   "B" = 3 points
   "C" = 2 points
   "D" = 1 point
   "F" = 0 points

   For example, if you took two classes, then those two grades will be averaged. This average is your G.P.A.

4) **If Maria took two classes last semester and earned an "A" and a "B," what is her G.P.A. for that semester?**

   Her "A" earns Maria four points

   Her "B" earns Maria three points

   So, I add those up:

   4 + 3 = 7

   Then, divide that total by the number of classes, which is two in this case.

   So,

   7/2 = 3.5

   Maria's G.P.A. for that semester is **3.5**.

5) **What's a "residency requirement"? How does it affect how much tuition you have to pay?**

Most state schools require students to be a resident of that county or city, depending on whether the school is funded by a county, city, or state tax. Students who are residents get lower-cost tuition than students who are non-residents.

6) **What's the difference between a certificate and a degree?**

A **certificate** is quicker to earn than a degree because it has fewer hours that a student must take. Most certificates take about a year and require about 30 credit hours.

A **degree** takes at least two years to earn and requires 60 or more hours, depending on which degree you get.

An **Associate's Degree** takes about two years to earn and requires about 60 credit hours.

A **Bachelor's Degree** takes about four years to earn and requires about 120 credit hours.

(This degree requires about four years **total**. If a student goes to a community college for the first two years, they transfer those hours to the university, and then they take two more years.)

Master's degrees, medical degrees, law degrees, and PhDs will require even more hours on top of the Bachelor's degree; how many hours and how long depends on the degree.

How long it takes to earn a certificate or degree depends on how many classes a student takes each semester. Part-time students will probably take a little longer to earn their credentials since they'll be taking fewer hours each semester.

Section II: Financial Aid

1) **Explain the differences between grants, loans, and scholarships.**

Grants, loans, and scholarships are all forms of aid to assist students in going to college.

Grants: Money (usually from the U.S. government) to go to school. It does not have to be paid back, as long as the student completes his classes and passes them.

Loans: Money (usually from the U.S. government) that must be paid back—with interest.

Scholarships: Money from various organizations given to a student for college. This form of aid almost never has to be repaid, as long as the student maintains the requirements of the scholarship (usually these requirements are making certain grades). If a student does not maintain the requirements, she may lose her scholarship.

2) **How do students apply for federal financial aid?**

Apply via the online F.A.F.S.A. form at fafsa.gov.

3) TRUE or FALSE:

Financial aid is an easy, punishment-free way to scam free money from the government. To do this, just pretend to enroll in college; then, once you get the money, you drop your classes, and keep your free money! The government will never catch you, and there won't be any repercussions later.

FALSE!

The U.S. government can and does track all students who accept money from them. There's plenty they can do to punish people who misuse this funding, including:

- Force the person to pay back the money they took
  - Garnishing wages
- Deny them financial aid in the future, until the money is repaid
- Ruin the student's credit rating
  - Bad credit ratings lead to reduced access to housing, higher interest and insurance rates, and denial of future credit

4) **TRUE or FALSE**

If you apply for financial aid, get approved, and then don't take the money, you'll get in trouble with the government.

FALSE!

Students apply for aid and then change their minds about using it all the time. If they already took the money, then they just give it back. If they haven't taken the money yet, they just don't accept it. They can always re-apply the next year, and there's no penalty.

Section III: Your Classes

1) **What is a "course schedule"?**

A course schedule is a list of all the classes a college offers. It tells students when and where the classes meet. It usually includes the instructor's name, campus, room number, and the date and time of class. (There may also be a link to the course syllabus and the textbook.)

2) **Where can students find their college's course schedule?**

Most colleges list their course schedule on their website. Students can also call the college's help line to find out where they can find the course schedule, and if a print copy is available.

3) **Explain what a "credit hour" is.**

A "credit hour" tells us how many credits we earn for completing the class and how many hours per week the class meets. For example, if a class meets three hours per week, then we'll earn three credit hours for completing it.

You can often tell the number of credit hours by looking at the course number. Usually, course numbers are three-digit numbers, and you can just look at that first number. For example, History 301 would earn us three credits, French 501 would earn us five credits, and Bio 402 would earn us four credits.

4) **About how many hours per week would you need to be able to take a three-hour college credit course? Be sure to include in your answer time for class, homework, and studying.**

It really depends. In general, most students need about *six hours per week total* for a three credit-hour class because they'll have to give three hours in class, and then another three hours for studying and homework.

However, the amount of time needed really depends on the class and the student's level of skill in that subject. For example, if I'm taking a science class that I find very difficult, then I might need seven or eight or even ten hours per week for that class. On the other hand, if I'm taking a math class that I find easy, I might only need five hours per week.

5) **Explain the difference between a "developmental course" and a "credit course."**

Developmental = course just below the college level; **does not** usually earn college credit

Credit course = college-level course; earns college credit

Students must pay for both, buy books for both, and study for both types of classes.

The main difference is that the developmental classes are designed to build student skills to the college level.

6) **TRUE or FALSE:**

Most professors prefer their students to be young and fresh out of high school.

FALSE!

Most professors couldn't care less about their students' ages. What the professor does care about is the students' overall behavior and attitude. When you're a professional, hardworking student who takes the class seriously, the professor will most likely adore you. Granted, there are a few crabby professors out there who won't like you no matter what you do, but happily these are rarities! Think less about your age and more about your behavior.

7) **In Chapter 10 of this book, we discussed the three-part process of preparing for tests. What were those three parts?**

Prep **before**, **during**, and **after** the test itself.

Before:
- Go to every class meeting and take lots of good notes
- Study the notes regularly—don't wait until the day before the test!
- Read all the chapters that will be covered
- See if the instructor will tell you *what kind* of test it will be (multiple choice, short answer, essay, etc.)
- Ask the instructor if she might make a review for the class

- Go to office hours and ask questions!
- Get a good night's sleep before the day of test
- Visualize yourself doing well on the test and say out loud, "I am going to ace this test!"
- Show up early on test day and eat a healthy meal

During

- Read the instructions!
- Scan the test and **answer the easiest items first**
- If it's a math test and you had to memorize formulas for it, write them down on your exam, if you are allowed
- Take a deep breath and do your best to stay calm
- Check the clock occasionally, so you know what time it is, but focus on testing, not on the time!

After

- When you get the test back, read over it to see what you got right and what you got wrong
- Look up the incorrect answers to be sure you understand why they're wrong
- Ask the professor if you have questions
- If you're allowed to keep the exam, then definitely keep it!
- Study old tests before the next one to remind yourself of this instructor's testing style
- Make notes on your studying methods. If you got an "A," then your study methods were successful, repeat!! If not, try new methods
- Talk to other students and find out who got an "A"; ask if they'll share their secrets!

8. **TRUE or FALSE:** A syllabus is like your rule book for your classes; it spells out what the rules are and what is expected of you as a student. It also usually outlines how to get an "A" or "B" in the course.
   TRUE!
   The syllabus outlines the rules and expectations for the class, including participation level required. It will also likely spell out how to earn each letter grade.

9. **Name some ways to save money on textbooks.**
   - Buy used books
     - Thrift store
     - Half-price bookstores
     - Half.com
     - Craigslist
     - Other students
   - Get an older edition
   - Rent books
   - Check libraries for your books
   - See if the school offers a textbook lending program

10. **List some of the ways we discussed to manage your time successfully.**
    - Be more conscious about how you spend your time
        - Try the 24-hour plan and declare war on time wasters
    - Make a schedule and stick to it, to see if it works
        - If not, be flexible and try new strategies until you find some that work for you
    - Try combining activities to save time, but just be sure that the activities you combine work well with each other
        - For example, trying to study while you spend time with three young children probably will not work, but walking while listening to recorded class lectures probably would work!

11) **Brainstorm below some ways that you might try to get family and friends to support your decision to go back to school.**
    Answers will vary here, but perhaps you said something such as:
    - Remind them of how going to school will help you—and how it will help them, too
    - Let them know they are still important to you and a college credential won't change that
    - Offer them the same support for **their** dreams
    - Schedule time with them so they know they're still in your life and that you love them—and make it *quality* time. Be present

Appendix F
(For Instructors) Sample Course Syllabus

Course Syllabus: College Success

Instructor: Office:

Email: Office Hours:

Course Description

This course will improve students' learning, self-management principles, and study strategies to increase their success in college. It provides an overview of key aspects, knowledge, and skills needed in the transition to college life. Students will identify their educational goals, personal strengths, and areas for development; become familiar with college resources and services; and explore strategies for academic success such as time management, study skills, and test taking. Students will also use Blackboard and other online learning tools to ensure familiarization with online learning.

Course Purpose: Facilitate students' transition into and success in college—and beyond...

Course Student Learning Outcomes

Upon successful completion of this course, students will:

1. Be oriented to the college experience.
2. Assess their current expectations, motivation, strengths, and areas for improvement.
3. Learn a process for and engage in setting effective academic, personal, and career goals.
4. Become familiar with college support services and resources.
5. Demonstrate their skills in self-management for successful outcomes.
6. Explore and apply essential learning and study skills for college-level work.

Instructional Methodology

This course will include the following teaching and learning methods: lecture, individual application exercises, small group activities, class discussions, online workshops and assessments, and homework assignments.

Texts/Materials
Required Book:
College Success for Adults: Insider Tips for Effective Learning by C.M. Gill

Recommended Texts/Materials:
Books:
What Color is Your Parachute? by Richard Nelson
Essential Writing Skills for College and Beyond by C.M. Gill

Supplies:
Pens/Pencils
Highlighters (Any color(s))
Spiral notebook or loose-leaf paper
Binder or folder
1 package colored index cards
Calendar/planner—either paper-based or an e-version (such as the one offered within your student Gmail account, or you may have a calendar function in your phone/tablet)

Classroom Climate

Learning takes place best in a setting where there is respect, positive regard, and freedom from distraction. It is my responsibility and intention to provide these conditions during the semester, and I will need your help to do so. Therefore, please make every effort to:

- Provide only respectful, honoring feedback
- Arrive to class on time and stay for the entire period
  - If you are late, take a seat quietly and do your best not to disrupt the class
  - If you need to leave early, please do so quietly and without disrupting
- Refrain from talking while another student or the instructor is speaking
- Keep your phone off or silent and out of sight (in your bag or purse); don't use it in class
- Arrive to class with all work completed and be ready to learn
- Respect your fellow learners and the class overall

Class Participation

Each student is strongly encouraged to participate in class. When participating in class discussions, keep in mind that the college classroom is one of the most diverse spaces within our society. Thus, you need to understand that there will be other members of the class with whom you disagree or who will disagree with you. This is fine; in fact, it is welcome. It is only through considering the beliefs and ideas of those with whom we disagree that we can truly decide on what we believe.

So, feel free to disagree with, refute, and/or challenge the ideas of others. However, when doing so, remain calm, polite, and respectful at all times toward your classmates, instructor, and their ideas. Anyone who shouts, engages in discrimination and/or vulgarity, or who is disrespectful in any way will be promptly dismissed and will receive an absence for the day.

Scholastic Honesty

Acts prohibited by the College for which discipline may be administered include scholastic dishonesty, including but not limited to cheating on an exam or quiz, plagiarizing, and unauthorized collaboration with another in preparing outside work. Academic work submitted by students shall be the result of their thought, research, or self-expression. Academic work is defined as—but not limited to—tests, quizzes (whether taken electronically or on paper), projects (either individual or group), classroom presentations, and homework. The penalty for violation of this policy will be determined by the instructor and could result in an "F" in the course.

Course Requirements

The following percentages will be used to determine final course grades:

1. Attendance/Participation—20%
2. General Homework Completion—20%
3. Journal Completion (5 total)—10% (2% each)
4. Quiz Completion—10%
5. Reflection Papers (3 total)—20% (6.67% each)
6. Mid-Term: 5%
7. Office Hours Visit: 5%
8. Final Exam: 10%

Extra Credit

Students may earn extra credit by applying to three scholarships this semester. (Bring proof of submission!) Your extra credit assignment (a 100, if completed) can replace your lowest grade—so long as *all* assignments in the course so far have been turned in complete and on-time.

Only students achieving the required 85% (or higher!) attendance and participation rates are eligible for extra credit.

**See Course Calendar on the following page for important dates and assignments.

COURSE CALENDAR

Date	Topics	Homework
Week 1	• Introductions & Welcome (Ice Breaker Games—with prizes!) • Syllabus Overview • Develop the Mindset of the Successful College Student	• Read Introduction and Ch. 1 in *College Success for Adults* • **Mindset Post Quiz Due** • **Paper #1 (Mindset) Due**
Week 2	• Top College Myths Debunked • Understanding the Value of an Education • Mastering the College Environment Part I: Understanding the Rules and Vocabulary	• Read Ch. 2 & Appendix A (College Vocabulary) in *College Success for Adults* • **College Myths Quiz Due** • **Journal #1 Due** • **College Vocab Quiz Due**
Week 3	• Choosing a Major and Degree/Certificate • Scam Schools, Diploma Mills, and Accreditation • Writing Essays for College	• Read Ch. 3 in *College Success for Adults* • **2 Career Assessment Quizzes Due (FOCUS2, MAPP, Myers Brigg, O*NET, etc.)** • **Paper #2 Due (Career Path)**
Week 4	• Understanding College Financial Aid (Loans, Grants, Scholarships) • Financial Aid Advisers Come to Class!! • Complete F.A.F.S.A. • Budgeting for College	• **Bring tax information for F.A.F.S.A. to complete in class with advisers!** • Read Ch. 4 in *College Success for Adults* • **Finish F.A.F.S.A., if need be** • **College Financial Budget Plan Due** **Reminder:** *Office Hours Visit Due by Week 10!*
Week 5	• Mastering the College Environment Part II: Professors' Expectations of Students • Top Strategies for selecting the Best Classes and Professors • "Holds" on Student Accounts—and Strategies to Clearing Them • **Special Guest Visitors from Student Services!**	• Read Ch. 5, 6, and Appendix H ("Beware the Bureaucracy") *in College Success for Adults* • **Tentative Class Schedule for Next Semester Due!** • Bring proof of: a) **All holds removed from Student Service** OR b) **Appointment with advisers to work on removing holds**

(Continued)

(Continued)

Date	Topics	Homework
Week 6	• Achieving Work/Life Balance • Time Management Strategies	• Read Ch. 7 in *College Success for Adults* • **Learning Styles Quiz Due!** • **24-Hour Exercise Due!** • **Time Management Plan Due!** ***Reminder:*** *Office Hours Visit Due by Week 10!*
Week 7	• Note-Taking Strategies for Success in College • Successful Study Strategies	• Read Ch. 8 in *College Success for Adults* • **Journal #2 Due** • **Note-Taking Quiz Due!** • **3 Note-Taking Samples Due!** • **Study for Mid-Term!**
Week 8	• Review for Mid-Term!! • **Mid-Term Exam!**	• Review all chapters read so far! • **Sample Mid-Term Due!** ***Reminder: Extra Credit Opp:*** Read Appendix C in *College Success for Adults* and apply to 3 scholarships!
Week 9	• Test-Taking Strategies • Overcoming Test Anxiety • Mastering Learning Technology	• Review returned mid-term • Read Ch. 10 & 11 in *College Success for Adults* • Schedule Office Hours visit, if you have not already! • **2 Posts to Discussion Board Due on Blackboard!** • **Journal #3 Due—submit via Blackboard!**
Week 10	• Help Services and Resources Available to the Contemporary College Student • Special Visitors: Office of Dean of Students, Student Life, and Library Services!	• Read Ch. 12 in *College Success for Adults* • **Paper #3 Due (Your Persistence Plan)** • **Office Hour Visit Due!** • **Help Chart Due!**
Week 11	• Job vs. Career • Career Search Strategies • Soft Skills • Special Visitors: Career Services! • Earning promotions and awards at work	• Read Ch. 13 & 14 in *College Success for Adults* • **Journal #4 Due** • **Journal #5 Due** • **Study for Final Exam!**

(*Continued*)

Date	Topics	Homework
Week 12	• Review • **FINAL EXAM!** • Course Evaluations • End-of-Semester Celebration	• **Sample Final Exam Due!** • **Complete "College Knowledge Quiz" in *College Success for Adults* (Appendix F)** • Last chance for ***Extra Credit:*** Read Appendix C in *College Success for Adults* and apply to 3 scholarships!

Bibliography

"America's Wars." *U.S. Department of Veteran Affairs*: Office of Public Affairs, https://www.va.gov/opa/publications/factsheets/fs_americas_wars.pdf. Accessed 3 January 2020.

"Avoiding Student Aid Scams." Federal Student Aid: U.S. Department of Education, https://studentaid.gov/resources/scams#identify-scam. Accessed 5 August 2019.

"Basic Eligibility Criteria." Federal Student Aid: U.S. Department of Education, https://studentaid.gov/understand-aid/eligibility/requirements. Accessed 5 August 2019.

"Beginning College Students Who Changed Their Majors within 3 Years of Enrollment." *U.S. Department of Education*, NCES 2018–434, December 2017. https://nces.ed.gov/pubs2018/2018434.pdf. Accessed 3 August 2019.

"Beyond Our Solar System: Stars, Galaxies, Black Holes, and More." *NASA Science Solar System Exploration.* https://solarsystem.nasa.gov/solar-system/beyond/overview/. Accessed 2 January 2020.

"California Community Colleges: Key Facts." *California Community Colleges*, https://www.cccco.edu/About-Us/Key-Facts. Accessed 16 January 2020.

Carnevale, Anthony P., Nicole Smith, and Jeff Strohi. "Learning While Earning: The New Normal." Georgetown University Center on Education and the Workforce, 2015, https://cew.georgetown.edu/wp-content/uploads/Working-Learners-Report.pdf. Accessed 4 August 2019.

Carnevale, Anthony P. Carnevale, Stephen J. Rose, and Ban Cheah. "The College Payoff: Education, Occupations, Lifetime Earnings." *Georgetown University*: The Center on Education and the Workforce, 5 August 2011, https://cew.georgetown.edu/cew-reports/the-college-payoff/.

Casciaro, Tiziana and Miguel Sousa Lobo. "Competent Jerks, Lovable Fools, and the Formation of Social Networks." *Harvard Business Review*, June (2005): 1. https://hbr.org/2005/06/competent-jerks-lovable-fools-and-the-formation-of-social-networks

"Casualty Status." U.S. Department of Defense, 27 January 2020, https://www.defense.gov/casualty.pdf. Accessed 30 January 2020.

Chang, Winni. "Grit and Academic Performance: Is Being Grittier Better?" *A* Dissertation, University of Miami, 2014.

Cilluffo, Anthony. "Five Facts about Student Loan Debt." Pew Research Center, 13 August 2019. https://www.pewresearch.org/fact-tank/2019/08/13/facts-about-student-loans/. Accessed 14 September 2019.

Clark, Kim. "How Much Money Should I Borrow for College?" *U. S. News & World Reports*, 9 June 2009, https://www.usnews.com/education/best-colleges /paying-for-college/articles/2009/06/09/how-much-money-should-i-borrow-for -college. Accessed 4 August 2019.

"Continue to Meet Eligibility Criteria." Federal Student Aid: U.S. Department of Education, https://studentaid.gov/understand-aid/eligibility/staying-eligible#sat isfactory-academic-progress. Accessed 4 September 2019.

Coren, Stanley. "You Can Teach an Old Dog New Tricks." *Psychology Today*, 24 February 2016, https://www.psychologytoday.com/blog/canine-corner/201602/ you-can-teach-old-dog-new-tricks. Accessed 12 May 2019.

Daggett, Stephen. "Cost of Major U.S. Wars." Congressional Research Service, 29 June 2010, https://fas.org/sgp/crs/natsec/RS22926.pdf. Accessed 4 January 2020.

Daly, Mary C., and Leila Bengali. "Is It Still Worth Going to College?" Federal Reserve Bank of San Francisco, 5 May 2014, https://www.frbsf.org/economic -research/publications/economic-letter/2014/may/is-college-worth-it-education -tuition-wages/. Accessed 19 May 2019.

"Demographic Characteristics of Undergraduates." *National Center for Education Statistics, U.S. Department of Education*, 1 September 2015, https://nces.ed.gov/ pubs2015/2015025.pdf. Accessed 7 June 2019.

Dryden, John, translator. *The Aeneid. By Virgil*. Harvard Classics, 1909.

Duckworth, Angela. *Grit: The Power of Passion and Perseverance*. Scribner, 2016.

Duckworth, Angela Lee, and Patrick D. Quinn. "Development and Validation of the Short Grit Scale (Grit–S)." *Journal of Personality Assessment*, vol. 91, no. 2, 2009, pp. 166–174. doi:10.1080/00223890802634290.

Dweck, Carol S. *Mindset: The New Psychology of Success*. Ballantine, 2006.

"Employment Projections." Bureau of Labor Statistics, United States Department of Labor, 4 September 2019, https://www.bls.gov/emp/ep_chart_001.htm. Accessed 15 January 2020.

Feldman, David B., and Diane E. Dreher. "Can Hope be Changed in 90 Minutes? Testing the Efficacy of a Single-Session Goal-Pursuit Intervention for College Students." *Journal of Happiness Studies*, vol. 13, no. 1, 2012, pp. 745–759. doi:10.1007/s10902-011-9292-4.

Franek, Rob. "Top 10 College Majors." *Princeton Review*, 2019, https://www.pri ncetonreview.com/college-advice/top-ten-college-majors. Accessed 20 June 2019.

"Frequently Asked Questions about Community Colleges." *U. S. News and World Report*, 9 July 2019, www.usnews.com/education/community-colleges/articl es/2015/02/06/frequently-asked-questions-community-college. Accessed April 2019.

Gates, Bill. "Help Wanted: 11 Million College Grads." *GatesNotes: The Blog of Bill Gates*, 3 June 2015, https://www.gatesnotes.com/Education/11-Million-College -Grads. Accessed 2 January 2020.

Grant, Heidi, and Carol S. Dweck. "Clarifying Achievement Goals and Their Impact." *Journal of Personality and Social Psychology*, vol. 85, no. 3, 2003, pp. 541–553. doi:10.1037/0022-3514.85.3.541.

Gregorian, Vartan. "The Myth of the Millionaire College Dropout." *Time*, 21 October 2011, http://ideas.time.com/2011/10/21/the-myth-of-the-millionaire-c ollege-dropout/. Accessed 14 April 2019.

"Grit." *Angeladuckworth.com*, January 2020, https://angeladuckworth.com/qa/. Accessed 16 January 2020.

"Helpful Job Shadow Questions." *Marquette University Career Services Center*, Marquette University. https://www.cals.vt.edu/content/dam/cals_vt_edu/alumni/mentoring/Job-Shadowing-Questions.pdf. Accessed 3 October 2019.

Hess, Frederick. "Old School: College's Most Important Trend is the Rise of the Adult Student." *The Atlantic*, 28 September 2011, www.theatlantic.com/business/archive/2011/09/old-school-colleges-most-important-trend-is-the-rise-of-the-adult-student/245823/. Accessed 14 June 2019.

"Job Growth and Education Requirements through 2020." *Georgetown University Center on Education and the Workforce*, 26 June 2013, https://cew.georgetown.edu/cew-reports/recovery-job-growth-and-education-requirements-through-2020/. Accessed 19 January 2020.

Kerr, Emily. "How to Avoid Scholarship Scams." *U.S. News & World Reports*, 1 April 2019, https://www.usnews.com/education/best-colleges/paying-for-college/articles/2019-04-01/how-to-avoid-scholarship-scams. Accessed 20 August 2019.

"Keyboard Shortcuts in Windows." *Microsoft.com*: *Windows Support*, 8 January 2020, https://support.microsoft.com/en-us/help/12445/windows-keyboard-shortcuts. Accessed 20 January 2020.

Leonhardt, David. "Bill Gates, College Drop-Out: 'Don't Be Like Me.'" *The New York Times*, 3 June 2015, https://www.nytimes.com/2015/06/04/upshot/bill-gates-college-dropout-dont-be-like-me.html?_r=0. Retrieved 14 April 2019.

"Mac Keyboard Shortcuts." *Apple Support*, 5 December 2019, https://support.apple.com/en-us/HT201236. Accessed 20 January 2020.

Metcalfe, Janet. "Learning from Errors." *Annual Review of Psychology*, vol. 68, no. 1, 2017, pp. 465–489. doi:10.1146/annurev-psych-010416-044022.

"More Employers Finding Reasons Not to Hire Candidates on Social Media, Finds CareerBuilder Survey." *Career Builder*, 27 June 2013, https://www.careerbuilder.com/share/aboutus/pressreleasesdetail.aspx?ed=12%2f31%2f2013&id=pr766&sc_cmp1=cb_pr766_&sd=6%2f26%2f2013&siteid=cbpr. Accessed 12 June 2019.

Mueller, Pam A., and Daniel M. Oppenheimer. "The Pen Is Mightier Than the Keyboard: Advantages of Longhand Over Laptop Note Taking." *Association of Psychological Science*, vol. 25, no. 6, 2014, pp. 1159–1168. doi:10.1177/0956797614524581.

Rojas, Joanne P. "The Relationships among Creativity, Grit, Academic Motivation, and Academic Success in College Students." (2015). Theses and Dissertations—Educational, School, and Counseling Psychology, 39, University of Kentucky, https://uknowledge.uky.edu/edp_etds/39. Accessed 20 January 2020.

Rubenking, Neil J. "The Best Antivirus Protection for 2020." *PCMag*, 3 January 2020, https://www.pcmag.com/picks/the-best-antivirus-protection. Accessed 17 January 2020.

Schlegel, Alexander A, Justin J. Rudelson, and Peter U. Tse. "White Matter Structure Changes as Adults Learn a Second Language." *Journal of Cognitive Neuroscience*, vol. 24, no. 8, 2012, pp. 1664–1670.

Sgroi, Daniel. "Happiness and Productivity: Understanding the Happy-Productive Worker." Global Perspectives Series: Paper 4. Social Market Foundation, October 2015, www.smf.co.uk/wp-content/uploads/2015/10/Social-Market-Foundation

-Publication-Briefing-CAGE-4-Are-happy-workers-more-productive-281015.pdf #page=9. Accessed 18 August 2019.

Singh, K., and Jha, S. D. "Positive and Negative Affect, and Grit as Predictors of Happiness and Life Satisfaction." *Journal of the Indian Academy of Applied Psychology*, vol. 34, no. Spec Issue, pp. 40–45.

Smith, Ashley A. "Degrees Lead on Wages." *Inside Higher Ed*, 29 March 2017, https://www.insidehighered.com/news/2017/03/29/wages-earnings-increase-sign ificantly-associate-degree-holders. Accessed 17 August 2019.

Snyder, C. R., et al. "Hope and Academic Success in College." *Journal of Educational Psychology*, vol. 94, no. 4, 2002, pp. 820–826. doi:10.1037/0022-0663.94.4.820.

"Some Burglars Using Social Media to Find Targets, I-Team Survey Shows." *NBC News: New York*, 22 August 2016, https://www.nbcnewyork.com/news/local/ investigations-i-team-social-media-use-survey-new-york-new-jersey/1329983/. Accessed 2 January 2020.

Straumsheim, Carl. "Decision Time." *Inside Higher Ed*, 24 August 2016, https:// www.insidehighered.com/news/2016/08/24/study-finds-students-benefit-waiting -declare-major. Accessed 8 February 2020.

Strayhorn, T. L. "What Role Does Grit Play in the Academic Success of Black Male Collegians at Predominantly White Institutions? *Journal of African American Studies*, vol. 18, no. 1, 2014, pp. 1–10. doi:10.1007/ s12111-012-9243-0.

Torpey, Elka. "High-Wage Occupations by Typical Entry-Level Education, 2017." *Bureau of Labor Statistics. The United States Department of Labor*, January 2019, https://www.bls.gov/careeroutlook/2019/article/high-wage-occupations.h tm. Accessed 14 May 2019.

Trostel, Philip. "It's Not Just the Money: The Benefits of College Education to Individuals and to Society." Lumina Foundation, 14 October 2015, https://ww w.luminafoundation.org/files/resources/its-not-just-the-money.pdf. Accessed 12 December 2019.

"Unemployment Rate 2.1 Percent for College Grads, 3.9% for High School Grads." *The Economics Daily*, 12 September 2018, https://www.bls.gov/opub/ted/2018 /unemployment-rate-2-1-percent-for-college-grads-3-9-percent-for-high-school-grads-in-august-2018.htm?view:full. Accessed 11 October 2019.

Venit, Ed. "How Late is Too Late? Myths and Facts about the Consequences of Switching College Majors." *Educational Advisory Board*, 23 August 2016, www .luminafoundation.org/resources/consequences-of-switching-college-majors. Accessed 15 September 2019.

Wenger, Jennie, Caolionn O'Connell, and Linda Cottrell. "Examination of Recent Deployment Experience across the Services and Components." RAND Corporation, 2018, https://www.rand.org/pubs/research_reports/RR1928.html? adbsc=social_20180320_2212921&adbid=975928167633334272&adbpl=tw &adbpr=22545453, Accessed 10 January 2020.

"Yesterday's Non-Traditional Student is Today's Traditional Student: Fact Sheet" *CLASP.org*, 14 January 2015, https://www.clasp.org/publications/fact-sheet/ yesterdays-nontraditional-student-todays-traditional-student-nontraditional. Accessed 14 May 2019.

Zimmer, Robert. "The Myth of the Successful College Dropout: Why It Could Make Millions of Young Americans Poorer." *The Atlantic*, 1 March 2013, www.theatl antic.com/business/archive/2013/03/the-myth-of-the-successful-college-dropout -why-it-could-make-millions-of-young-americans-poorer/273628/.Accessed   14 April 2019.

Zwettler, Clara, et al. "The Relation between Social Identity and Test Anxiety in University Students." *Health Psychology*, vol. 5, no. 2, 2018, pp. 1–7. doi:10.1177/2055102918785415.

Index

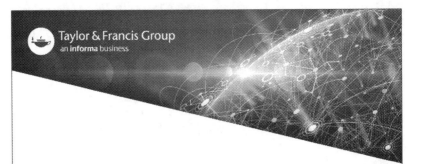

Printed in the United States
by Baker & Taylor Publisher Services